In the Spirit of Our Age

In the Spirit of Our Age | Eric Mendelsohn's B'nai Amoona Synagogue

Kathleen James-Chakraborty

MISSOURI HISTORICAL SOCIETY PRESS

St. Louis

Published in collaboration with the Center of Contemporary Arts

Special financial support provided by Ken and Nancy Kranzberg and Furthermore, the publication program of The J.M. Kaplan Fund.

© 2000 by the Missouri Historical Society. All rights reserved.
Published in the United States of America by the Missouri Historical Society Press
P.O. Box 11940, St. Louis, Missouri 63112-0040

Printed in Canada

04 03 02 01 00   5 4 3 2 1

Library of Congress Cataloging-in-Publication Data

James-Chakraborty, Kathleen, 1960–
In the spirit of our age: Eric Mendelsohn's B'nai Amoona synagogue/
Kathleen James Chakraborty.
p. cm.
Includes bibliographical references.
1. Congregation B'nai Amoona (Saint Louis, Mo.) 2. Saint Louis (Mo.)–Buildings, structures, etc. 3. Mendelsohn, Erich, 1887-1953–Criticism and interpretation. 4. Architecture, Modern–20th century–Missouri–Saint Louis. I. Title.

. — ISBN 1883982-32-4.

NA5235.S67 J36 2000
00-055446

726'.3'092–dc21
CIP

This paper meets the requirements of the American National Standard for Permanence of Paper for Printed Library Materials, Z39.48-1992

Book and Jacket Design by: Patricia Boman Design, St. Louis
Cover photograph of the Center of Centemporary Arts building, formerly the B'nai Amoona Synagogue, by Gen Obata, 2000.
Photograph, this page, by Gen Obata, 2000.
Printed and Bound by: Friesens, Altona, Manitoba, Canada

Distributed by Syracuse University Press

In memory of Meyer "Mickey" Kranzberg (15 November 1905–15 November 1977),

vice president of B'nai Amoona during its construction

and first president of the completed synagogue.

Contents

Acknowledgments	ix
In the Spirit of Our Age	1
B'nai Amoona: Portrait of a Client	11
Eric Mendelsohn Meets St. Louis	17
Symphony in Steel: Design and Construction	24
House of God; House of the People; House of the Torah	40
A Place in History?	49
Epilogue	67
Notes	70
Portfolio by Gen Obata	77

Acknowledgments

No project this extensive is a solitary effort. I am delighted to have the opportunity to thank the multiple communities that have encouraged me to undertake and complete this examination of the architecture of the former B'nai Amoona and present Center of Contemporary Arts (COCA). I have made many friends in the process, which have rewarded me personally and professionally.

From the moment she first contacted me to find out if I would be interested in organizing an exhibit about B'nai Amoona, Linda Skrainka has provided the impetus for the book's realization. Her enthusiasm has been unflagging, as has the hospitality that she and her husband, Steve, have graciously extended on multiple occasions. COCA's Stephanie Riven and her husband, Roger Goldman, have also been generous hosts, while Stephanie's stewardship of the building and the style in which she directs the institution it now houses have been an inspiration throughout. My thanks extend to her staff and to the whole COCA family.

In St. Louis, four other groups of people have facilitated my research. First and foremost are the families of those who built B'nai Amoona in the first place. I. E. Millstone kindly met with me twice to share his memories of the building that so completely reflects his extraordinary talents. The Ferer, Kranzberg, and Spitzer families agreed to numerous interviews, which provided great insight into the congregation and its history. Peter Winston also assisted me in understanding Mendelsohn's connections in St. Louis. Next to acknowledge are the staffs of the many local institutions that have preserved information about the building and its history, as well as the rich local context of modern architecture. Jan Barron kindly gave me access to B'nai Amoona's archives, including photographs of the building in use. The staffs of the St. Louis Art Museum, St. Louis Jewish Community Archives, St. Louis Public Library, and Missouri Historical Society were also unfailingly helpful. A number of people contributed greatly to my understanding of the region and its architecture. I am particularly indebted in this regard to Esley Hamilton, Stephen Leet, Eric Mumford, and Eric Sandweiss. Final thanks go to Lee Sandweiss, Josh Stevens, and the staff at the Missouri Historical Society Press, whose excitement about the project greatly facilitated the production of this catalog; to Gen Obata, whose exquisite photographs capture the enduring beauty of B'nai Amoona; and to Patricia Boman, whose beautiful design elegantly complements Mendelsohn's work.

Elsewhere in the United States, a number of people helped me understand the architectural climate in America's postwar Jewish community. Cynthia Field, Walter Leedy, Jared Serwer, and Susan Solomon were very helpful in this regard, particularly by giving me access to unpublished research, enabling important insights.

B'nai Amoona's architect, Eric Mendelsohn, was born in Germany, where I researched at the Kunstbibliothek in Berlin. The staff went out of its way to help me complete my work in the institution's Mendelsohn Archive. Fellow Mendelsohn scholars Ita Heinze-Greenberg and Regina Stephan contributed their insights after reading an early draft of the manuscript. Last, but by no means least, Sumit Chakraborty and, as ever, Friedegund Holzmann provided the friendship that nurtured and sustained me as I wrote.

The production of the exhibition "Architect of Form and Spirit: Eric Mendelsohn in St. Louis," September 2000–March 2001, at the Center of Contemporary Arts, and of the book *In the Spirit of Our Age: Eric Mendelsohn's B'nai Amoona Synagogue*, published by the Missouri Historical Society Press in conjunction with the exhibition, received support and assistance from many individuals and organizations. The Center of Contemporary Arts would like to extend special thanks to Ken and Nancy Kranzberg and Furthermore, the publication program of The J.M. Kaplan Fund, for their support of this catalogue. In addition, COCA would like to acknowledge Terry and Gordon Bloomberg; Bob Dubinsky; John and Yvette Dubinsky; Helen and Gene Kornblum; Stephen W. and Linda Dubinsky Skrainka; DaimlerChrysler Corporation Fund; Graham Foundation for Advanced Studies in the Fine Arts; Hellmuth, Obata + Kassabaum; Missouri Arts Council; Missouri Historical Society; National Endowment for the Arts; Regional Arts Commission; University City Committee for Access and Local Origination Programming with a fund established in cooperation with TCI Cablevision.

1882   Sixtieth Jubilee   1942

Our Dream Has Come True.
מזל טוב!

Our Dream of years is to become a Reality, with the help of God.

Just as we go to press we are happy to announce that we have purchased the South East Corner of Trinity and Washington Avenue, University City, where we hope to erect the New B'nai Amoona Synagogue.

Congregation B'nai Amoona

In the Spirit of Our Age | Eric Mendelsohn's B'nai Amoona Synagogue

1 "Our Dream Has Come True!" page from *B'nai Amoona Sixtieth Jubilee, 1882–1942* (St. Louis, 1942). Source: St. Louis Jewish Community Archives, Saul Brodsky Library, St. Louis County, Missouri.

2 United Hebrew Temple (now the Missouri Historical Society Library and Research Center), Maritz and Young with Gabriel Ferrand, 1924, St. Louis. Source: Missouri Historical Society, St. Louis.

In 1942 B'nai Amoona, St. Louis's leading Conservative Jewish congregation, published a Jubilee volume celebrating its sixtieth anniversary. In it, the congregation declared that "just as we go to press we are happy to announce that we have purchased the South East Corner of Trinity and Washington Avenue, University City, where we hope to erect the New B'nai Amoona Synagogue."[1] The announcement was illustrated with a sketch of a building whose prominent dome was capped by a Star of David (fig. 1). The design clearly resembled the architecture of other nearby synagogues, notably United Hebrew, located a mile to the south, and Shaare Emeth, located just across Washington Avenue from B'nai Amoona's new site (fig. 2). These two synagogues, both housing Reform congregations, had led the steady movement westward of St. Louis's Jewish institutions from their historic locations in the city's central and near-north neighborhoods. United Hebrew moved to its neo-Byzantine quarters on Skinker Boulevard in 1924; Shaare Emeth erected its new home in the adjacent suburban community of University

3 B'nai Amoona Synagogue (now the Center of Contemporary Arts), Eric Mendelsohn, 1945–50, University City, Missouri. Source: Mendelsohn Archive, Staatliche Preussische Kunstbibliothek, Berlin.

City in 1932.[2] Yet, the building that B'nai Amoona finally dedicated in 1950 was radically different from the original sketch. Deviating from the conventional motif that had distinguished prosperous American synagogues from churches for most of the first half of the twentieth century—including the classical or Byzantine domes that evoked the Jewish faith's Middle Eastern origins—this was a startlingly modern building (fig. 3). No trace of ornament interrupted the exquisitely balanced play of masses that gave the building its character and culminated in the great sweep of the curved cantilever that roofed the sanctuary.

What had happened in the eight years separating B'nai Amoona's first conventional rendering and the completion of the first modernist synagogue in the United States? How did an established synagogue in the Midwest end up initiating a national trend of architectural experimentation among postwar Jewish congregations? The answers to these questions lie in the conjunction of four separate stories, two local and two international in scope. These trends will form the backdrop of the more detailed story that follows and can be summarized briefly at the outset.

1. Local Migration   In St. Louis itself, the steady westward movement of the city's population was epitomized by the migration of the city's sizable Jewish community, which historically had clustered in the neighborhoods of the central corridor, between the predominantly German-Irish north and south sides. As local Jews prospered and the population of the region grew, synagogues followed their congregations to the western edges of the city and beyond. Even before the construction of Shaare Emeth, University City—just west of the city limits—was becoming the center of the region's Jewish community. In St. Louis, as in so many American cities, suburbanization was a gradual and continual phenomenon, taking place through the entire twentieth century rather than in one explosive postwar push.[3] Indeed, by 1942 B'nai Amoona's leadership already lived west of the new site.[4] University City was the heart of Jewish life in the region in the early postwar years. Other buildings constructed in the community included the Yalem branch of the Jewish Community Centers Association, the Yeshiva Reb Zachariah Joseph, and three synagogues: Chesed Shel Emeth, Shaare Zedek, and Nusach Hari B'nai Zion.

4

2. Modernism in St. Louis

While Jews—like many St. Louisans—moved west into newer suburbs, the St. Louis area quietly became a center for architectural experimentation. The decades of the 1930s, '40s, and '50s were marked by the construction of a series of buildings—located in and around the city and its suburbs—that remain of more than regional importance. From Harris Armstrong's groundbreaking Shanley Building in Clayton of 1935—one of the most sophisticated examples of the International Style erected in the Midwest in the thirties—through the work of William Bernoudy, Frederick Dunn, Samuel Marx, Joseph Murphy, Charles Nagel, Gyo Obata, Eero Saarinen, and Minoru Yamasaki, local architects and their counterparts from around the country collaborated to make the region a showcase for new thinking about architecture. In their works, historical references increasingly gave way to the soaring feats of engineering and the structural aesthetic of the Gateway Arch, Lambert Airport, and Priory Chapel (fig. 4). This progressive architectural climate encouraged Eric Mendelsohn, one of the founders of the modern movement in Europe, to hope to settle in the city (fig. 5).[5]

4 Gateway Arch, Jefferson National Expansion Monument, Eero Saarinen, 1948–65, St. Louis. Source: Missouri Historical Society.

5 Eric Mendelsohn. Source: Mendelsohn Archive.

3. Eric Mendelsohn: A Career in Transition

Although Mendelsohn moved in 1945 from the New York area to San Francisco instead of to St. Louis, his ties to St. Louis architects Marx, Nagel, and Murphy, as well as the presence in the city of his former patron Erwin Weichmann (later Winston), ultimately brought this extraordinary architect to the attention of B'nai Amoona. Mendelsohn had gained international renown with the publication in 1921 of the images of the Einstein Tower (fig. 6). Located just outside of Berlin, this startling building housed an observatory and laboratory for research into relativity. He also published widely read books on the architecture of the United States, which he visited in 1924, and the Soviet Union, where he built a factory. Mendelsohn eventually became one of Germany's, and Europe's, most successful architects during the twenties, designing factories, department stores, office buildings, and an influential cinema. As a Jew and a Zionist, he left the country quickly after Hitler seized power in 1933, settling first in London and then in Jerusalem before coming to the United States in 1941. After four difficult years of merely lecturing around the country and working for the war department, Mendelsohn acquired B'nai Amoona as his first American commission and the first of the four synagogues that would compose his most important contribution to American architecture.[6] Along with a never-realized design for a Holocaust memorial in New York's Riverside Park, these buildings also indicated a strong commitment to supporting Jewish life and memory in his adopted homeland (fig. 7).

6

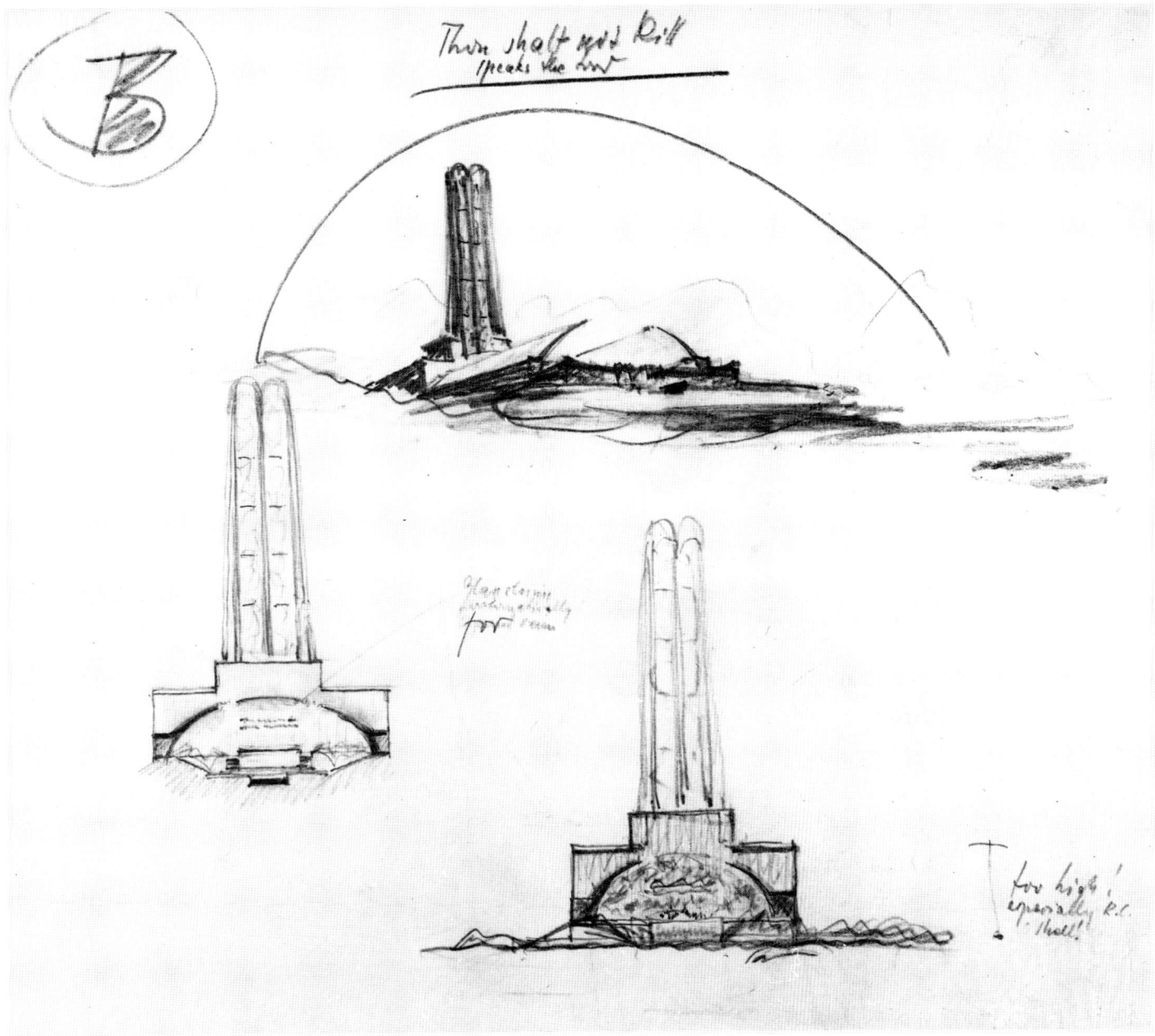

6 Einstein Tower, Mendelsohn, Potsdam, Germany, 1920–21. Source: *Erich Mendelsohn*: *Das Gesamtschaffen des Architekten: Skizzen, Entwürfen, Bauten* (Berlin: Rudolf Mosse Verlag, 1930), 45.

7 Memorial to the Six Million Jewish Victims of the Nazis, Mendelsohn, proposal for Riverside Park, New York City, 1950–52. Source: Mendelsohn Archive.

4. The Rise of a Modernist Religious Architecture

Mendelsohn's own arrival in America, together with the traumatic upheaval of the Holocaust, coincided with a broader trend: the reconsideration of the principles of religious architecture. Within this widespread movement, Mendelsohn set out to reinvent the synagogue to fulfill the specific needs of postwar American Jews. Many American Jews feared that assimilation would weaken the bonds that remained between the survivors of the recent destruction of the European communities; in response, Mendelsohn intended B'nai Amoona and the buildings that followed it to encourage Jews, and particularly Jewish children, to socialize together. Consequently, B'nai Amoona and its successors featured assembly halls, classrooms, offices, and kitchens, as well as the sacred space of the sanctuary. The spirit of the building was equally important to Mendelsohn, which reflected his long-standing admiration for American political institutions. In a 1947 article titled "In the Spirit of Our Age," he commented:

Thus our temples should reject the anachronistic representation of God as a feudal lord, should apply contemporary building styles and architectural conceptions to make God's house a part of the democratic community in which he dwells. Temples should reject in their interiors the mystifying darkness of an illiterate time and should place their faith in the light of day. The House of God should either be an inspiring place for festive occasions that lift up the heart of man, or an animated gathering place for a fellowship warming men's thoughts and intentions by the fire of the divine word given forth from altar and pulpit right in their midst.[7]

Like many of its Conservative counterparts around the country in the 1920s, B'nai Amoona had been the first Jewish congregation in St. Louis to conceive of the synagogue as a community center. In 1950 the construction of such a facility in a patently modern style was entirely new in the United States. It is not surprising that Mendelsohn embraced this challenge. Already in Germany he had erected a number of facilities for Jewish communities, ranging from cemetery chapels in Allenstein and Königsberg to a social lodge in Tilsit and a youth center in Essen.[8] Furthermore, the last of these had been located close to churches by Otto Bartning and Dominikus Böhm. This pair of German-Christian architects had pioneered a community-based approach to the construction of churches, one whose emphasis on constructional drama corresponded with Mendelsohn's own predilections.

Although the emergence of the modern movement in architecture is usually identified with building types more obviously expressive of a new machine age—above all, factories and workers' housing, but also exhibition halls, bridges, department stores, and office buildings—such innovative religious structures fit squarely within a more human strain of the modernist movement evident in Europe and the Americas since at least the 1920s. Far more than the architecture championed by Henry-Russell Hitchcock and Philip Johnson as the International Style, this more humanized approach accounted for the widespread popularity of modern architecture during the forties and fifties, when its association with an egalitarian social model flourished. Because these developments still occupy the shadowlands of architectural history, however, the importance of such buildings as B'nai Amoona rarely has been recognized, except by those who in the first years after its completion addressed the state of contemporary American synagogue design.

Each of the forces that brought B'nai Amoona's new building into being—the Jewish community of St. Louis, the city's disposition towards modern architecture, the career of its architect, and the development of a modern religious architecture—ultimately was transformed by its presence. This landmark building served as a beacon of what modern architecture could contribute, both to St. Louis and more broadly to the American Jewish community. If these lessons often have been forgotten in subsequent years, the fiftieth anniversary of the building's dedication provides a fitting occasion for remembering the optimistic fusion of religion, engineering, and democracy that Eric Mendelsohn and the congregation of B'nai Amoona tried to form.

B'nai Amoona: Portrait of a Client

8 B'nai Amoona (presently Holy Metropolitan Baptist Church), Alfred Meyer, St. Louis, 1918–19. Source: B'nai Amoona, Town and Country, Missouri.

Although attention usually focuses on the architect, the client is equally important to the creation of almost any building. It was, for instance, the members of B'nai Amoona who decided to hire Mendelsohn, ensuring that they would get an unusual and in many ways experimental building. Also, it was they who raised the money to erect most of what he had originally designed and stuck by him through cost overruns. Who were the men and women who supported such a daring design?

B'nai Amoona ("children of faith" in Hebrew) was founded sometime before 1884, probably by immigrants from Cracow. As St. Louis's only German-speaking Orthodox congregation, it attracted a large and upwardly mobile membership, many of whom eventually joined Reform temples. In 1917 Abraham Halpern was appointed rabbi. A graduate of the Jewish Theological Seminary in New York, Halpern led B'nai Amoona into the Conservative movement, a new middle ground between Reform and Orthodox Judaism. Halpern, whose tenure at B'nai Amoona lasted until 1962, placed a strong emphasis on education.[9] In 1918 he declared, "The greatest asset of any Synagogue is the school. If our children be given the proper Jewish training, made to understand what the Jewish religion is, and its value, we would soon find that instead of our children leaving us, they would remain with us."[10] From the beginning, Halpern developed the community-oriented infrastructure at B'nai Amoona that was characteristic of Conservative congregations during the interwar years, one that would form the basis for all of Mendelsohn's synagogues.[11]

Throughout its history, B'nai Amoona has been, like many synagogues, a peripatetic institution.[12] In 1884 the congregation rented facilities at Fourth Street and Washington Avenue in the heart of downtown; three years later they moved to 823 Franklin Avenue. The following year the congregation paid $10,000 to purchase the First German Baptist Church located just northwest of downtown at the corner of Thirteenth and Carr Streets. In 1906 the synagogue moved west again, this time into the former Central Presbyterian Church on the northwest corner of Garrison and Lucas Streets. The church's new quarters had been built in 1876 at the cost of $145,000, but with the decline of the neighborhood, B'nai Amoona paid only $30,000 for it. Only eleven years later, B'nai Amoona itself abandoned the building, which they sold for $22,000 to an African American congregation.[13]

B'nai Amoona's adaptive reuse of old buildings was typical of early Orthodox congregations in the United States.[14] When in 1914 Shaare Zedek became the first Orthodox congregation in St. Louis to erect its own building, B'nai Amoona quickly followed that ambitious example. Designed by Alfred Meyer, B'nai Amoona's new home at Academy and Vernon in the city's West End was dedicated in 1919 (fig. 8). The actual architecture of the new synagogue was unremarkable. Little distinguished the outward appearance of the building from that of a church, which allowed for the building's eventual conversion into the Holy Metropolitan Baptist Church. Grand architectural gestures—whether Islamicist, as was common in the second half of the nineteenth century, or neoclassical and Byzantine, as became typical in later years—remained almost exclusively the purview of Reform congregations.[15] New, at least for St. Louis, was the range of facilities eventually added to the complex. A school and library next door were completed in 1921, and three years later a second expansion provided more facilities for the congregation's growing programs. Halpern intended these activities to bind members together socially and thus facilitate the continued practice of their faith.[16]

The continued movement westward of the B'nai Amoona's increasingly prosperous members, however, threatened its success. The synagogue always had been located in working- and lower-middle-class neighborhoods, but during the 1920s many of its members moved into resolutely middle-class University City, where for the first time they could exchange their apartments and row houses for ample detached homes set on tree-shaded lots. In 1936 congregants resolved to buy a site for a new building, and despite a delay caused by the depression, they purchased the Xenia United Presbyterian Seminary at the corner of Trinity and Washington Avenues, a block south of University City's monumental civic center. They altered its two buildings to serve as temporary quarters and made plans to replace one with a new building as quickly as possible.[17]

The B'nai Amoona's Jubilee volume, published for the synagogue's sixtieth anniversary, paints a compelling portrait. Despite having led B'nai Amoona away from strict Orthodoxy, Halpern stressed the compatibility of tradition with the social activism that would form one of his major bonds with Mendelsohn:

> Other Congregations of the city and the country may be older but we have remained faithful to the Traditions of our fathers, that have been the very strength of our religious way of life. Nor have we overlooked the great ideals of social justice and the prophetic emphasis of these ideals. These are all part of Traditional Judaism, but we haven't neglected those Traditions that have given warmth and beauty to Jewish life. . . . We too are fully cognizant of the Prophetic emphasis on the way of life through which we can rise to the glorious heights of moral and ethical grandeur but we also know that the dignity of Jewish living and Jewish survival has been made possible through those Traditions that added body to the spirit of our ideals. To us our ritual and social ideals are interwoven, each giving beauty and meaning to the other.[18]

Halpern and the other contributors to the anniversary volume were only too aware, however, of the war then raging in Europe and of the implications for the Jewish people. Although many among the congregation's leadership remained wary of Zionism, the congregation as a whole embraced this cause, declaring, "In that little land [of Israel] we look for the rehabilitation of our homeless people, and in that little land we look for the reawakening of the great spiritual truths through which humanity can find the peace that we are seeking."[19] The themes struck by the volume's nationally prominent contributors would shape the face of postwar Judaism for B'nai Amoona and for similar congregations across the country. Albert Einstein bluntly stated the threat: "In the past we were persecuted despite the fact that we were the people of the Bible; today, however, it is just because we are the people of the Book that we are persecuted. The aim is to exterminate not only ourselves but to destroy, together with us, that spirit expressed in the Bible and in Christianity which made possible the rise of civilization in Central and Northern Europe."[20] Abram Sachar, director of the Hillel Foundation, worried that "some of the best brains in Jewish life have become so concerned with world issues that they have completely lost their concern with Jewish survival," the best hope for which, he believed, lay in democracy. He wrote that democracy "alone protects the sanctity of the individual, the right of group uniqueness, and above all, the principal of equality of opportunity," although he also noted the importance of economic security to society.[21]

It was, however, Israel Goldstein, president of the Synagogue Council of America, who best understood the responsibilities American Judaism would face after the war. Goldstein preached the importance of developing new forms of cultural expression to meet those responsibilities:

Now the finger of Providence points to American Israel as the "saving remnant." It is necessary, first, that we should recognize that upon us devolves the responsibility of carrying the torch of the Torah which has fallen from the hands of European Jewry. Ours becomes now the difficult but glorious privilege of keeping alive the sacred flame which from ancient Palestine moved to the academies of Babylonia and thence successively to Spain, France, Germany, Poland, and Russia. Are the Jews of America prepared to bear their fateful responsibility today?

American Jewry has come of age physically, economically, and philanthropically. It stands on its own feet as a strong, free and relatively affluent community. American Jews have not as yet, however, come of age, culturally and spiritually. It has been thus far a spiritual and cultural dependency, dependent upon Jewish inspiration furnished by European scholarship and devotion to the Torah. It must now develop its own spiritual and cultural resources and moreover rise to the responsibility of serving as a fountain-head for Judaism in the Western Hemisphere as a whole. We here must compensate for the losses sustained by Judaism abroad.

American Jewry needs greater spiritual and cultural content for its own sake as well. Without spiritual and cultural content, Jewish life in America is devoid of dignity, worth and meaning.[22]

This is the challenge that the congregants of B'nai Amoona would seek to meet when, just three years later, they hired Eric Mendelsohn to design their new synagogue.

9

10

9 Shop Interior, Weichmann silk store, Mendelsohn, Gleiwitz, Germany (now Gliwice, Poland),1922–23. Source: Peter Winston.

10 Interior of Weichmann apartment. Source: Peter Winston.

11 Interior of Weichmann apartment. Source: Peter Winston.

Eric Mendelsohn Meets St. Louis

11

Mendelsohn first visited St. Louis more than a year before he was contacted by B'nai Amoona. The purpose of his visit to the city in March 1944 was to deliver a lecture in the Liberal Forum, a series sponsored by the Young Men's Hebrew Association. The lecture may have been arranged through the auspices of Erwin Winston, who owned a local fabric store. Winston had immigrated to St. Louis from Gleiwitz, Germany (now Gliwice, Poland), in 1938. In the process, he had adopted the name Winston, in honor of the prominent British statesman, Winston Churchill, whose steadfast opposition to fascism he greatly admired.[23] As Erwin Weichmann, Winston had been one of Mendelsohn's earliest German clients. His silk store had been Mendelsohn's first such commission (fig. 9). Probably designed in collaboration with Richard Neutra, who worked as an assistant in Mendelsohn's office before emigrating to the United States in 1923, the building's strong horizontal accents reflect the admiration both Neutra and Mendelsohn had for Frank Lloyd Wright.[24] Above the shop were two apartments. One, initially occupied by Winston himself, was furnished largely by the Mendelsohn office (fig. 10 and 11). Winston later brought much of its contents with him to America.[25] The building served as an important precedent for the larger shops and department stores that became one of Mendelsohn's greatest contributions to the development of modern architecture.

12

After the lecture was scheduled, Mendelsohn worked through multiple channels to maximize its local impact. Key to his efforts was his successful attempt to bring to the St. Louis Art Museum (then still the City Art Museum) the exhibition of his work organized three years earlier by the Museum of Modern Art in New York. This showcase, sponsored by the institution identified most closely with the dissemination of a modern architectural style in the United States, provided a vital opportunity for the emigré architect to establish his reputation in America. Unfortunately, its opening on 3 December 1941, was followed just four days later by the Japanese bombing of Pearl Harbor and the subsequent American entry into World War II.[26] Although the exhibit consequently had little impact in New York, it did nonetheless help give direction to Mendelsohn's activities during the war years. In 1942 the exhibit traveled first to the Arts Club in Chicago and then to the San Francisco Museum of Art (now the San Francisco Museum of Modern Art). The San Francisco exhibit provided the occasion for a series of three lectures at the University of California, Berkeley. These later were published, and in 1948 Mendelsohn joined the Berkeley faculty as a lecturer.[27]

Both Victor Packman, a St. Louis lawyer, and Gilbert Harris, the executive director of the local YMHA, approached City Art Museum director Charles Nagel about the possibility of a Mendelsohn exhibit in St. Louis.[28] Nagel, a trained architect, proved receptive. In partnership with Frederick Dunn, Nagel had recently designed St. Mark's Episcopal Church in south St. Louis (fig. 12). This small building—erected at a cost of only $75,000—was the region's first religious structure designed in a modernist idiom, one that remained quite distinct, however, from the airy lightness that characterized the most experimental European architecture of the previous decade.[29]

The exhibit offered St. Louisans interested in modern architecture a portrait of the career of one of its principal exponents.[30] It opened with the fantastic drawings that Mendelsohn had executed during World War I (fig. 13). The original publicity material noted that "these sketches, which have been widely admired in architectural circles, form an important document of Expressionist architecture," although Mendelsohn, who always sought to distance himself from the utopian longings of expressionism's leading architectural exponent, Bruno Taut and his circle, excised the reference to expressionism.[31] Whatever stylistic label applied to them, these monumental industrial structures, to be built of steel and reinforced concrete, constituted one of the most radical visions of a new architecture proposed throughout the entire twentieth century. The structure contained not a hint of historical form or ornament, and the extraordinary plasticity of the designs, which seemed at times to defy gravity, captured Mendelsohn's excitement about the dynamism of modern life, a power that seemed almost to hurl them forward into space.[32]

12 St. Mark's Episcopal Church, Charles Nagel and Frederick Dunn, St. Louis, 1939. Source: Missouri Historical Society.

13 Factory with tower, Mendelsohn, project, 1917. Source: Mendelsohn: Gesamtschaffen, 60.

Visitors to the St. Louis exhibition likewise would have been struck by the multiple images of the Schocken Department Store in Stuttgart, 1926–28, and of Columbus House, a Berlin highrise completed in 1932 (figs. 14 and 15). Although modest in scale by American standards, these were among the largest structures yet realized in Europe by proponents of the modern movement. Furthermore, as forthright expressions of an industrial aesthetic they did not mask—as their American counterparts almost always did—the connection between the factory and the downtowns where its products were consumed. Finally, they were tailored exquisitely for their designated urban sites.

While Mendelsohn's celebrated German work formed the backbone of the St. Louis exhibition, more than half of the work exhibited dated from the eight years he had spent in London and Jerusalem before coming to the United States. Fifteen of the images depicted the Hadassah University Medical Center on Jerusalem's Mt. Scopus, of 1934–39 (fig. 16). The largest single work of Mendelsohn's entire career and the first of his three hospital designs, this commission marked a radical departure from the tautly curved and amply glazed skins of his best German and British work. Required by Jerusalem's building regulations to face the complex in local stone, Mendelsohn sought to balance an entirely modern

14

15

16

function—that of an up-to-date hospital—with respect for a city whose importance lay in its sacred past rather than an industrial present. The result was a building whose qualities of dignity and permanence replaced the dynamic curves and almost weightless cantilevers that had characterized his commercial architecture. Narrow windows controlled the entrance of the harsh desert light, while a trio of cupolas made respectful reference to local Arab architectural traditions.[33] Here, as in his later American buildings, Mendelsohn displayed sensitivity to place in the creation of an architecture that was resolutely ahistorical but not necessarily expressive of the industrial conditions that had driven so much of his earlier architecture.

The strength of the exhibition was just one reason why Mendelsohn found a cordial reception in St. Louis. Supported by Winston, the architect found his way paved, in part, by friend and fellow architect Samuel Marx, who already had been instrumental in bringing the Mendelsohn exhibit to his own hometown of Chicago.[34] Marx was related by marriage to Morton May, owner of the May Company and the Famous-Barr department stores. May's house in Ladue, designed by Marx, was one of the most prominent local examples of modern design. Additionally, Marx's May Company store in Los Angeles and the Famous-Barr store in Clayton, for which his firm had served as the associate architects, remain among the most important translations of Mendelsohn's commercial idiom (fig. 17).

14 Schocken Department Store, Mendelsohn, Stuttgart, Germany, 1926–28. Source: Mendelsohn Archive.

15 Columbus House, Mendelsohn, Berlin, Germany, 1931–32. Source: Mendelsohn Archive.

16 Hadassah University Medical Center, model view, Mendelsohn, Jerusalem, British Mandate of Palestine (now Israel), 1934–39. Source: Arnold Whittick, *Eric Mendelsohn* (London: Leonard Hill Limited, 1956), Plate 41c.

17 Famous-Barr Department Store, Mauren, Russell, Crowell and Mullgardt, with Samuel A. Marx, Nol L. Flint, and Charles W. Schonne, Associated Architects, Clayton, Missouri, 1948. Source: Missouri Historical Society.

17

Although he stayed in St. Louis only a few days, Mendelsohn made several key contacts. For instance, he participated on the art museum's radio program in a discussion of his work conducted with Joseph Murphy, a professor of architecture at Washington University who became a cherished colleague.[35] He also received favorable attention from the local newspapers, which his future clients at B'nai Amoona likely noticed. A photograph of Mendelsohn installing the exhibit appeared in the *St. Louis Star-Times*.[36] Undoubtedly more important was the *St. Louis Globe-Democrat*'s review, which praised the recent Near Eastern work, singling out the Hadassah hospital's "stark serenity of purpose" and labeling the stair in the house for Chaim and Vera Weizmann "a perfect jewel."[37]

Mendelsohn, in turn, was excited by St. Louis. Speaking to a group of architecture students, he praised Louis Sullivan's Wainwright Building as the city's most distinctive contribution to modern architecture.[38] He wrote his wife, Louise, about the city's rosy postwar prospects and its position between the European-oriented East Coast and the Asian-facing West.[39] Almost immediately Murphy and Packman mounted an attempt to capitalize on this enthusiasm by bringing the architect to the city permanently.

Mendelsohn dreamed of coming to St. Louis either as the recipient of a university chair in the architecture school at Washington University or as an advisor to the Board of Public Works. He explained his qualifications for the first, more conventional position, the equivalent of what Harvard had accorded Gropius or what Armour Institute of Technology (later the Illinois Institute of Technology) had bestowed upon Ludwig Mies van der Rohe:

My inborn understanding of the formative principles of contemporary architecture—the third structural revolution in history [following the Greek and the Gothic]—should from the very start eliminate the elementary uncertainty of today's architecture schools and the erratic experiments, blunders and superficialities of their work—quite unnecessary after nearly 100 years of creative achievements. In my opinion, an important factor in the expedite planning and visual appearance of America's post-war position and world influence.[40]

He also stressed the relevance of his recent experience in Mandate Palestine in a statement that highlighted his turn during the 1930s away from a machine-based aesthetic and towards one based on regional considerations:

> My agricultural background and acquaintance with domestic and public building in semi-tropical countries should promote the technological adjustment of all building activities to the geological, climatic and productive peculiarities of the twin-river States— a characteristic regional variety with the general orbit of contemporary American architecture.[41]

His interest in a position with the city was unusual in American terms, although in Germany this arrangement was common. It gave both power and prestige to those, such as Martin Wagner in Berlin during the twenties, who held such a position.

It took more than a year before it became clear that the university would not offer Mendelsohn the position he sought. In September 1945, however, B'nai Amoona building committee chair Sam Ferer contacted Mendelsohn. Failing to secure a job at Washington University and with the city government, Mendelsohn moved to San Francisco rather than St. Louis in November. However, he left B'nai Amoona, a concrete legacy of the warm welcome the midwestern city had extended to him at perhaps the most difficult time of his professional career. His appreciation had come in the form of the region's most dramatic new building.

Symphony in Steel: Design and Construction

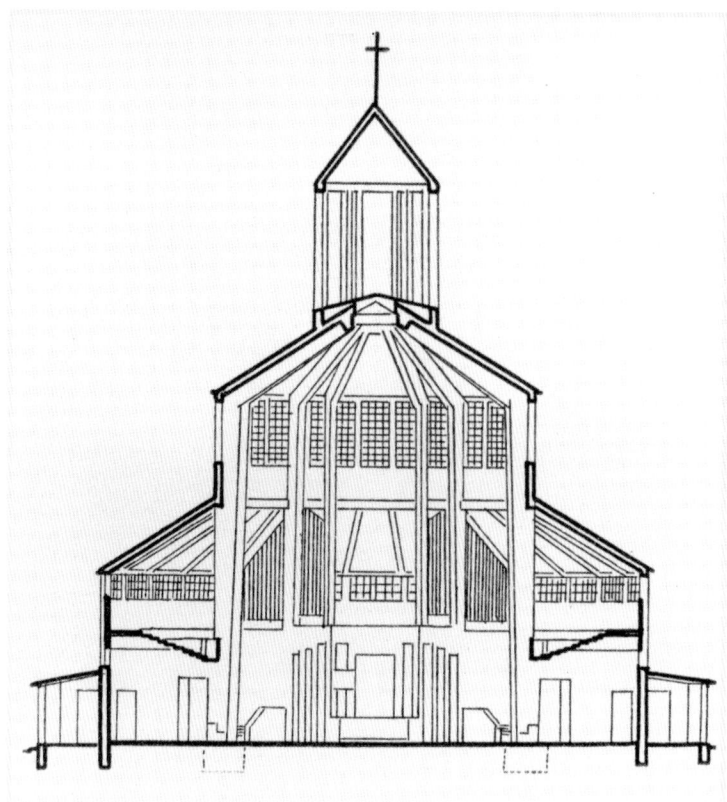

Mendelsohn returned to St. Louis in October 1945 to meet with members of the building committee; by November he had obtained the commission. Although the congregation initially anticipated moving into its new quarters in time for the 1947 High Holy Days, the project was delayed two years, with construction of its first phase completed in 1950.[42] In the interim, Mendelsohn experimented with transposing the Christian church architecture of Weimar Germany into his first synagogue design, the congregation was wracked by disagreements that highlighted their uncertainty over their identity, and rising construction costs frustrated all parties involved. In the end, however, both the architect and his clients were delighted by what the congregation's own publicity labeled "Our dream comes true."[43]

Mendelsohn described his October trip in a letter to his wife, Louise, whom he wrote almost daily. He was pleased particularly by Ferer, whom he rightly judged as capable of winning over the congregation. (The following year Mendelsohn would describe Ferer as "a man of the world, a charming host, and generous friend.")[44] Although he judged his first meeting with the building committee a "full success (no overstatement!)," he admitted that "as it is with committees, it will take them a little longer to decide."[45] Mendelsohn was not unrealistically optimistic. Within weeks he had received word that he had gained the commission but with two stipulations: that he have a local associate architect and that the cost of the new synagogue not exceed $350,000. Although initially leery of the first stipulation (eventually resolved by

18 Resurrection Church, Otto Bartning, 1930, Essen. Source: Ferdinand Pfammatter, *Betonkirchen: Voraussetzung, Entwicklung, Gestaltung* (Zurich: Binziger Verlag, 1948), 62.

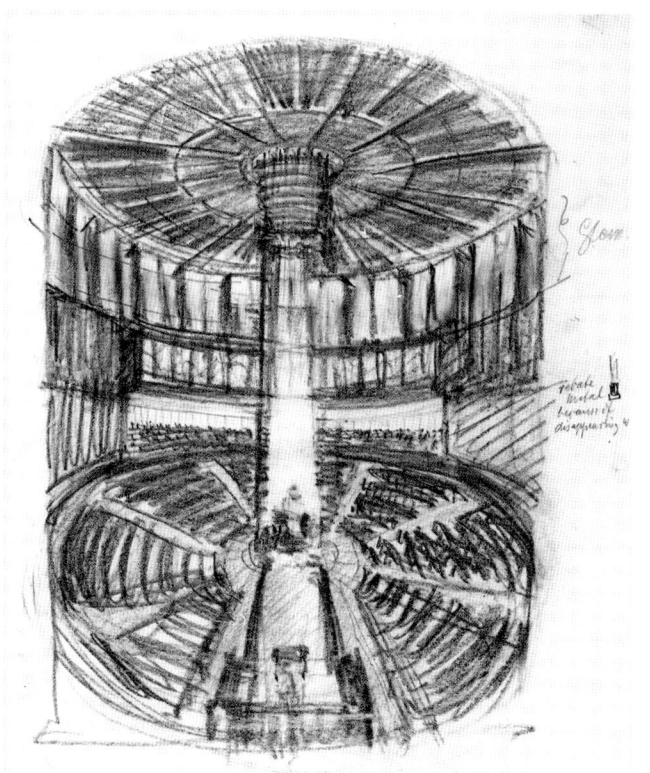

19 Preliminary Perspective of Interior, B'nai Amoona, 1945–46. Source: Mendelsohn Archive.

the appointment of Bernard Bloom), he accepted the second "on condition that I am free to change the building program accordingly."[46] Delayed by illness, Mendelsohn returned in December to confirm the details with the committee. At that point he agreed to a commission of 6 percent of construction costs, plus 1 percent for a check of the works. Plans and specifications were to be ready within four months; construction was to begin in six.[47]

Back in San Francisco, Mendelsohn began the task of designing his first American building. His first experiments illustrate the influence of his memories of the synagogues and churches of Germany, particularly those he had become familiar with while building the Jewish Youth Center in Essen. Both the synagogue in Essen—designed and built in a vaguely historicist style between 1911 and 1913 by Edmund Körner—and Bartning's Resurrection Church of 1930 had circular central spaces (fig. 18). Framed in concrete, the Resurrection, or Round, Church, was one of interwar Europe's boldest experiments in the creation of a dramatically new sacred form that bore the clear imprint of its decidedly modern materials: steel and reinforced concrete.[48] Mendelsohn also admired the work of Dominikus Böhm, whose St. Engelbert Church in the Cologne suburb of Riehl was another of the most dramatic churches completed in Germany before the Nazi takeover in 1933.[49] As his synagogue designs repeatedly would demonstrate, Mendelsohn shared Bartning and Böhm's conviction that structure, space, and light—rather than historical references or ornament of any kind—should establish the sacred quality of a place.[50]

Mendelsohn's earliest scheme was for a circular temple, as he always called the sanctuary, where the Torah ark—repository of the sacred scrolls—would be located against the wall, with the bima (the pulpit) at the absolute center (fig. 19). Cantilevered balconies would supplement the ground-floor seating.⁵¹ The surviving drawings of this preliminary design, which echoes the circular interior of the Essen synagogue and repeats many details of the internal layout of Bartning's nearby church, are extraordinary, as they offer a rare example of Mendelsohn thinking from the inside out.⁵² In contrast to his usual practice of beginning with exterior perspectives, he struggled—as is evident from eight of the fourteen drawings—with the design of the sanctuary, especially with the structure that he hoped would enable him to place a glazed oculus over the bima.

Compared to these almost fanatically detailed drawings, those of the exterior are quick sketches, establishing little more than his characteristic interest in dynamic massing. At this early stage, the architect apparently envisioned placing the temple at the corner of Trinity and Washington, where it could be spotted most clearly from Delmar Boulevard just to the north. As he experimented with replacing the previously circular sanctuary with a bold upward sweep (note the Star of David capping this scheme), Mendelsohn decided to shift the sanctuary to the southwest corner—the eventual location of the assembly hall (fig. 20).⁵³ The question now was what shape the temple would take in both plan and elevation.⁵⁴ Would it be circular or rectangular in plan with a flat or sloping roof (fig. 21)? Early plans for this arrangement show the assembly hall on the Trinity and Washington corner with the classrooms to the east and south (fig. 22).

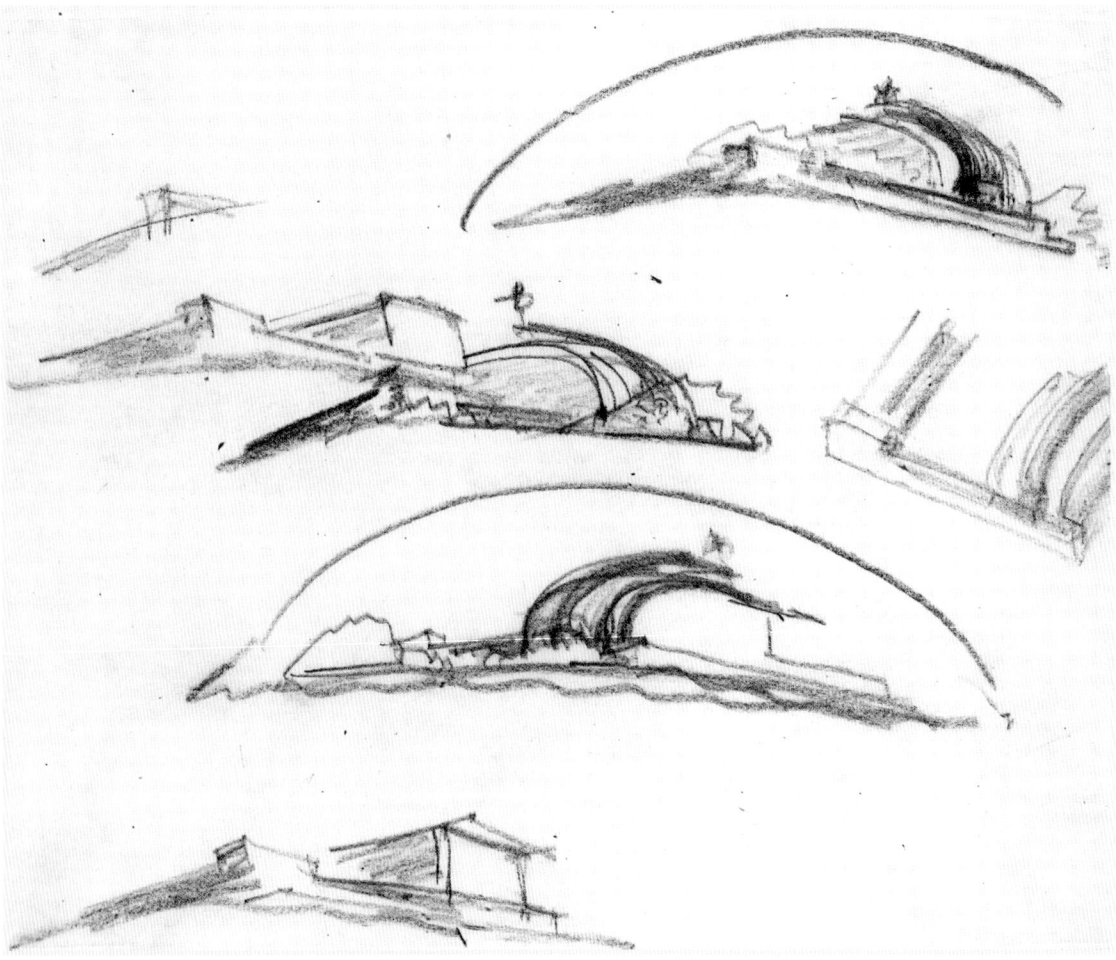

20

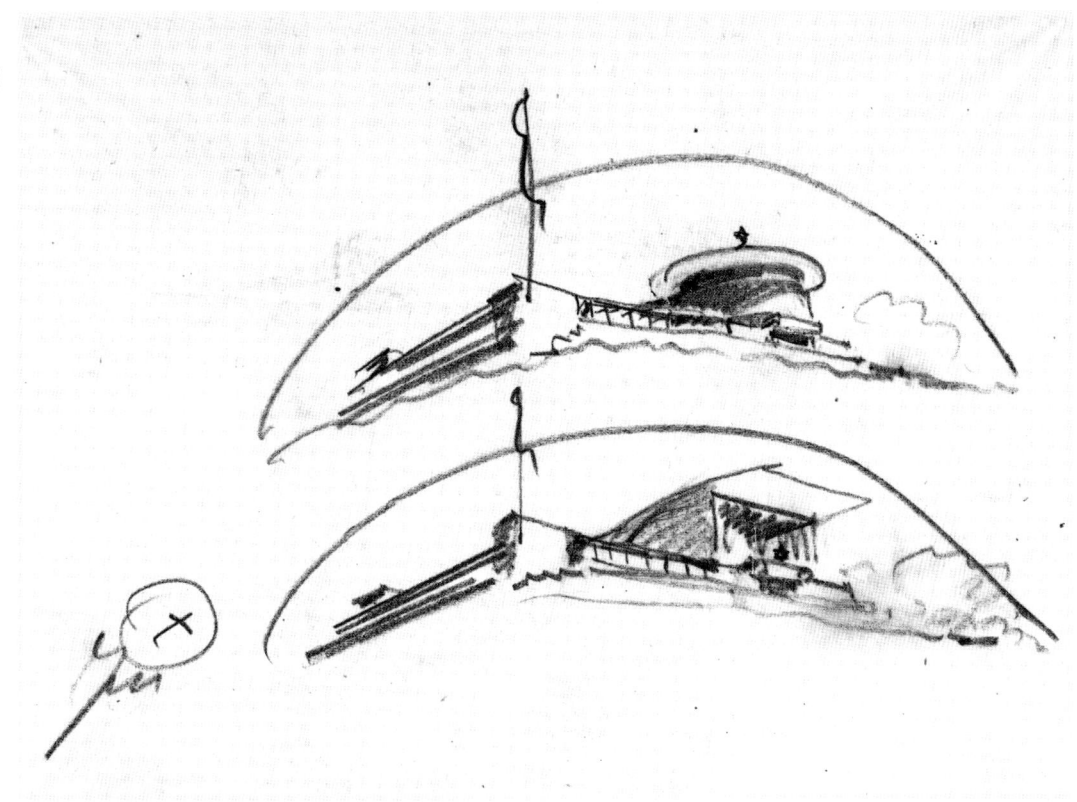

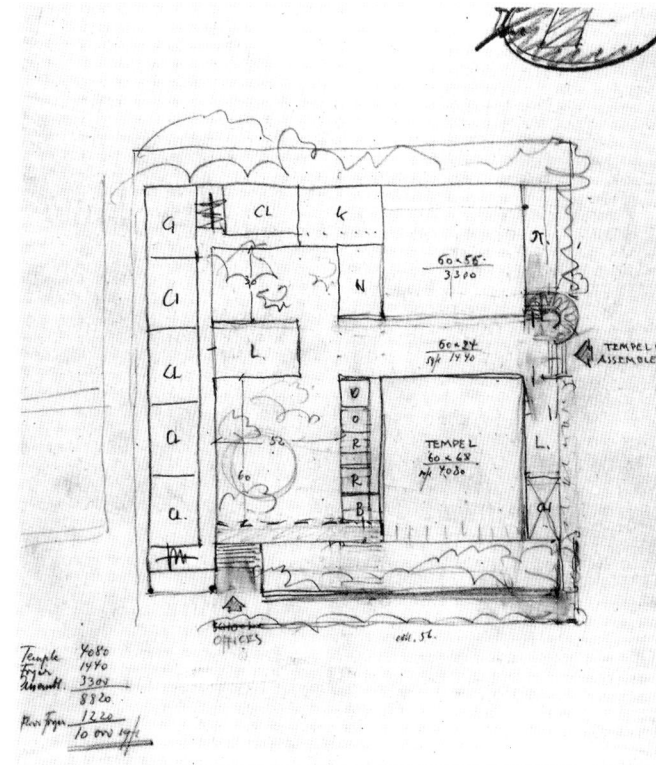

20 Preliminary Perspectives of Exterior, B'nai Amoona, 1946. Source: Mendelsohn Archive.

21 Preliminary Perspectives, B'nai Amoona, 1946. Source: Mendelsohn Archive.

22 Preliminary Plan, B'nai Amoona, 1946. Source: Mendelsohn Archive.

(In later plans, however, he located the assembly hall behind the temple [fig. 23].) Classrooms now lined the Washington and rear facades of the building, separated from the temple by a courtyard, where he inserted a library (fig. 24).[55] Finally, after having settled on its striking parabolic profile, Mendelsohn decided to switch the location of the assembly hall and temple once again, having the former face Trinity and placing the latter behind it to the east (fig. 25).[56] This design was probably the one he brought with him to St. Louis at the end of February (fig. 26).[57]

If the strongly sculptural mass of the building was characteristically Mendelsohnian, the particular form of this design was nonetheless quite specific to its function as a religious building. Mendelsohn undoubtedly was familiar with the way that Böhm had used parabolic arches during the twenties to create a modern medievalism that appeared to contemporaries as both timelessly primal and up-to-date. For Mendelsohn, as for Böhm,

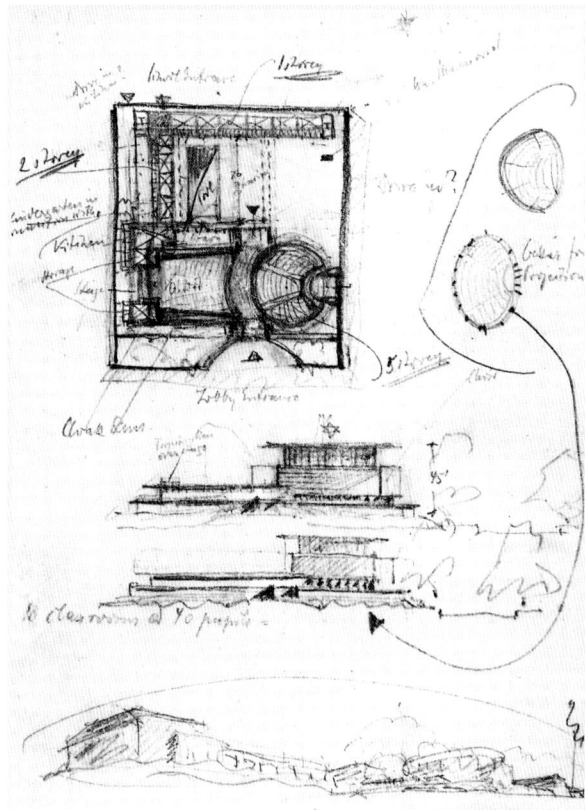

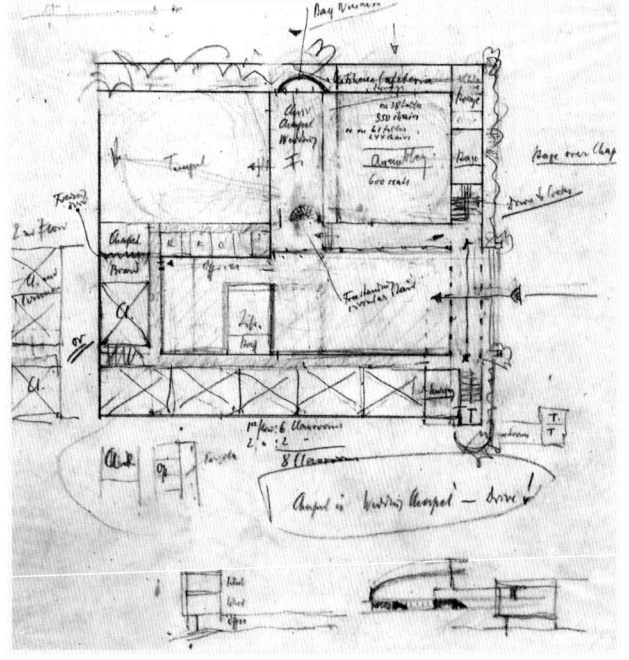

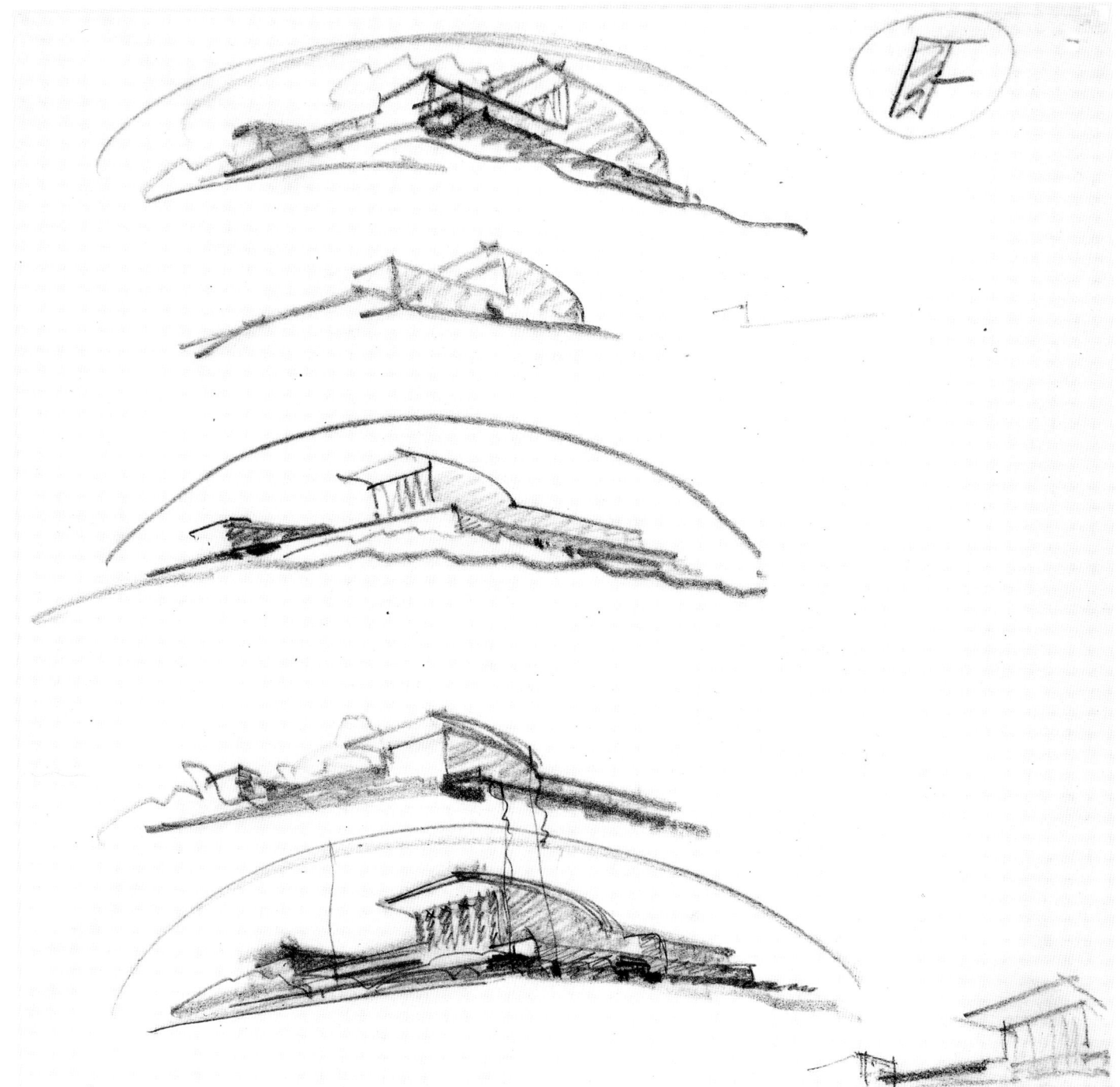

23 Preliminary Perspectives and Plan, B'nai Amoona, 1946. Source: Mendelsohn Archive.

24 Preliminary Plan and Section, B'nai Amoona, 1946. Source: Mendelsohn Archive.

25 Preliminary Perspectives, B'nai Amoona, 1946. Source: Mendelsohn Archive.

26 Perspective, B'nai Amoona, 1946. Source: Mendelsohn Archive.

the exploitation of modern structural principles was the key ingredient to the revitalization of outmoded traditions of sacred building. Mendelsohn once declared of B'nai Amoona that "its daring construction is proud—as the monumental buildings of all early historical periods were—to show its structural method as its formative principle."[58] Although Mendelsohn by no means imitated the specifics of St. Engelbert or any other Böhm church, it is difficult to conceive that he would have turned to the parabolic form without this example (fig. 27). Mendelsohn was best known for his dynamic curvilinear architecture, but none of his earlier buildings displayed upward-sweeping curves, as they do here. Only in his drawings for imaginary structures, especially those drawn at the beginning of his career, did he envision the architecture that he would realize in his American synagogues.

Undoubtedly, Mendelsohn surmised correctly that such unusual shapes would be easier to build in America, whose construction industry he long had admired as the world's most advanced. Even before he first saw them for himself in 1924, the enormous grain silos that lined the waterfront in Buffalo and Chicago had encouraged his search for dynamic forms (fig. 28). Nonetheless, his original interest in an industrial aesthetic largely had been eliminated from this experimentation with plastic form. Instead, the experience of the building—

27 St. Engelbert Church, Dominikus Böhm, Cologne-Riehl, 1930–32. Source: *Dominikus Böhm: ein deutscher Baumeister* (Regensburg: Josef Habel Verlag, 1943), 21.

and in this case the principle interior rather than the exterior—was now paramount. The very purpose of this plasticity was now different as well. Instead of celebrating a technology that they took for granted, the members of B'nai Amoona turned to Mendelsohn to provide them with spaces where they could nurture their faith and sense of community.

At first it appeared as if Mendelsohn indeed had done this. His initial meeting with the building committee went well. Only Frank Dubinsky refused to vote for acceptance of the design. Already, however, Mendelsohn warned that the "high price of labor and materials" would result in at least a 10 to 15 percent increase over the initial costs.[59] The meeting with the entire congregation was "stormy." Mendelsohn wrote his wife that "the reaction to my plans and model reflected the whole scale of human emotions—from the tears of the scholarly Rabbi to . . . base hatred."[60] As always, Ferer saved the situation.

28 Grain Silos and Distribution Bridge, Chicago. Source: Eric Mendelsohn, *Amerika: Bilderbuch Eines Architekten* (Berlin: R. Mosse, 1928), 42.

He "concluded that there are really only 2 ways open. Either we accept Mendelsohn's work as it is—progressive and exciting . . . or we pay off Mendelsohn—and appoint Dubinsky as our architect."[61]

For reasons that remain unclear, the task of drawing up plans and putting them out to bid went more slowly than originally expected. Mendelsohn did not work unassisted. When he moved to San Francisco in the fall of 1945, he entered a short-lived partnership with two young local architects, John Dinwiddie and Henry Hill. The firm's stamp is on many of the drawings for B'nai Amoona. Individual sheets were signed by a number of different draftsmen. The names given include Hansen, Hastings, Kruse, and Hans Schiller, who had immigrated to the United States from Israel to resume work for Mendelsohn. By 1949 Michael Gallis appeared on Mendelsohn's stamp as an associate architect, but although he worked closely on later synagogue designs, he appears to have made no significant contribution to the execution of B'nai Amoona. Clyde Bentley was the supervising engineer.[62]

Mendelsohn and his staff apparently began work in May, the date of the earliest surviving office drawings.[63] He was particularly busy with the design in June, when he revised many details of the basement and second-floor plans while also worrying about the situation in the Middle East. As usual, he listened to classical music as he sketched. He wrote his absent wife:

> This is just a short note after a day home with St. Louis interiors and Beethoven. Problems solved so far, to be ready for more. Profusely troubled by the events in Palestine. I despise the English, and don't need to have any dealings with them anymore. And I am afraid, this is only the beginning, a horrifying signal for the Arabs.[64]

When he submitted his drawings for bid, the project experienced its first crisis. Estimates came in at over $700,000, more than double the amount the congregation had hoped to spend.[65]

In Germany Mendelsohn's modern style had been inexpensive and efficient to construct. In the United States, he consistently underestimated the costs of his synagogue designs, which sometimes resulted in the drastic revision of his original schemes (Cleveland, Baltimore, and St. Paul) or contributed to the complete cancellation of the project (Washington and perhaps Dallas). Although some of the problem could be attributed to Mendelsohn's romanticization of the American construction industry, postwar inflation accounted for much of it. In St. Louis, almost all of Mendelsohn's original vision eventually would be realized after a divisive struggle within the congregation. The cost of the building's construction—met only because of the extraordinary generosity of leading members—would continue to weigh heavily on B'nai Amoona's finances for years to come.[66]

Mendelsohn returned to St. Louis in May 1947, but the results proved inconclusive.[67] The congregation rejected a set of substitute plans. From that point until they accepted yet another modified plan in March 1948, a battle over the site embroiled the membership.[68] Both Spitzer, the president of the congregation, and Ferer, the chair of the building committee, offered to resign before work resumed. At issue—more than the details of Mendelsohn's plans—was the general question of whether B'nai Amoona should even build on the Trinity Avenue site or instead purchase one farther to the west. Several different lots were under consideration. A prominent location at Clayton and Hanley Roads, in the suburb of Clayton, was rejected only after the cost proved too high. Another possibility was nearby at Westwood and Clayton, while a third—preferred by the majority of the board as well as Rabbi Halpern—was in the western reaches of University City at Westview and Delmar. Mendelsohn generously offered not to charge for the revisions necessary to erect the building on the third site. Eventually, however, the Westview location proved to have its own problems. Because the site was on a landfill, the congregation would have to spend $200,000 to drive the piles necessary for the foundations. By the time they realized this, the alternatives, which now included a site at Big Bend and Clayton Roads, were either unavailable or too expensive. At last, the congregation resolved to build on the property they already owned, provided the cost not exceed $500,000, a figure that quickly grew to $565,000 and ultimately entailed the elimination of the north, or classroom, wing.[69]

The debate over the site reflected the significant demographic changes taking place in the Jewish community. Many of the younger and wealthier members of the congregation correctly surmised that with continued postwar prosperity the region's Jewish community would continue to move steadily westward to newer and more prosperous suburbs. Settling several miles to the west of any previous synagogue would have ensured B'nai Amoona an even more central role in the flourishing community. Additionally, from an architectural perspective, several of these sites offered the opportunity to construct an even more prominent building, one set back on a broad green lawn from a major thoroughfare. In the end, issues of cost led the congregation back to the original site purchase. Also significant was the fact that Halpern had declared it kosher to ride the streetcar west on Saturdays from the neighborhood surrounding the previous synagogue to Trinity and Washington, while more outlying sites could be reached only by car.[70]

The ground breaking finally took place in September (fig. 29). It was a festive occasion, attended by local notables as well as most of the congregation.[71] As an article in the *Jewish Post* pointed out, costs had risen once again, but the congregation's faith that Mendelsohn would design them a celebrated structure was proving true:

Ground for a $750,000 temple, heralded as one of the most modern and advanced in America, will be broken at 11 A.M., Sunday, September 19. . . . [A]bout six months ago its architect completed the plans and they received acclaim in national architectural circles.[72]

29 Ground breaking, B'nai Amoona, 19 September 1948. Source: St. Louis Jewish Community Archives.

Not all commentators were so impressed, however. The *Post-Dispatch* called it merely "one of the most unusual structures of contemporary design." [73]

Construction was directed by a local contractor, Isadore E. Millstone, who, the building committee noted, "by winning over Mr. Mendelsohn on several matters is saving considerable money."[74] Millstone was assisted by his brother Edgar, who died, however, before the project's completion. I. E. Millstone had known Mendelsohn's work since his days as an architectural engineering student at Washington University. He and his firm played a crucial role in translating Mendelsohn's vision—based on somewhat idealized views of the American construction industry—into the reality of a finished building. Mendelsohn, like other European emigrés, came to the United States often with impractical notions about when to use steel. While he would propose this expensive material for the

frame of a modest house, as he had in his 1944 design for the Winston House in Clayton, he did not fully grasp its capacity to be molded efficiently into such complex forms as the great span over the sanctuary of B'nai Amoona. Already with a national reputation for expertise in steel-reinforced concrete, Millstone and his firm were situated ideally to persuade Mendelsohn to use steel for the sanctuary. In addition, the Millstones deftly executed details, even meeting conditions set by Mendelsohn that they regarded as unnecessary and problematic, such as his refusal to lay beams upon the concrete floor slab, which made setting the steel mullions into the slab quite tricky.[75]

Mississippi Structural Steel crafted the frame of the sanctuary. The six curved 140-foot-long I-beams, which taper as they rise, were finished on site.[76] Watching them being put into place provided the greatest drama of the construction process (fig. 30), as a congregation fund-raising brochure described:

30

It was breath-taking to see the steel frame work rise to the great heights and reach the majestic scope that our new Synagogue has taken. It was like a great symphony whose diverse instruments produce the harmony that is soothing to the ear and delighting to the soul. The same effect was experienced as one gazed at the ten-ton girders being set into position, and which stand at the support of the entire structure. It was truly a symphony in steel. Then the concrete was poured, and the walls rose, and the steel frame took on shape and form. It was like the Prophet Ezekiel's vision in the valley of the dry bones. We are told that God said to the Prophet: "Behold I will lay sinews upon you, and will bring flesh upon you, and I will cover you with skin, and put breath into you and ye shall live.[77]

As construction continued, Mendelsohn spent more time on the details of the interior and particularly of the sanctuary, which, while proposing his design to the congregation, the architect had depicted in two stunning perspectives (fig. 31). Almost entirely absent from his earlier projects, such spec drawings would become hallmarks of his attempts to explain his designs to the large number of people responsible for implementing their construction.[78] In 1947 he wrote his wife regarding the possible commission for a synagogue in Washington, D.C., that "I experienced again that it has no value to depict an unconventional project just from plans, elevations, and very sketchy perspectives."[79]

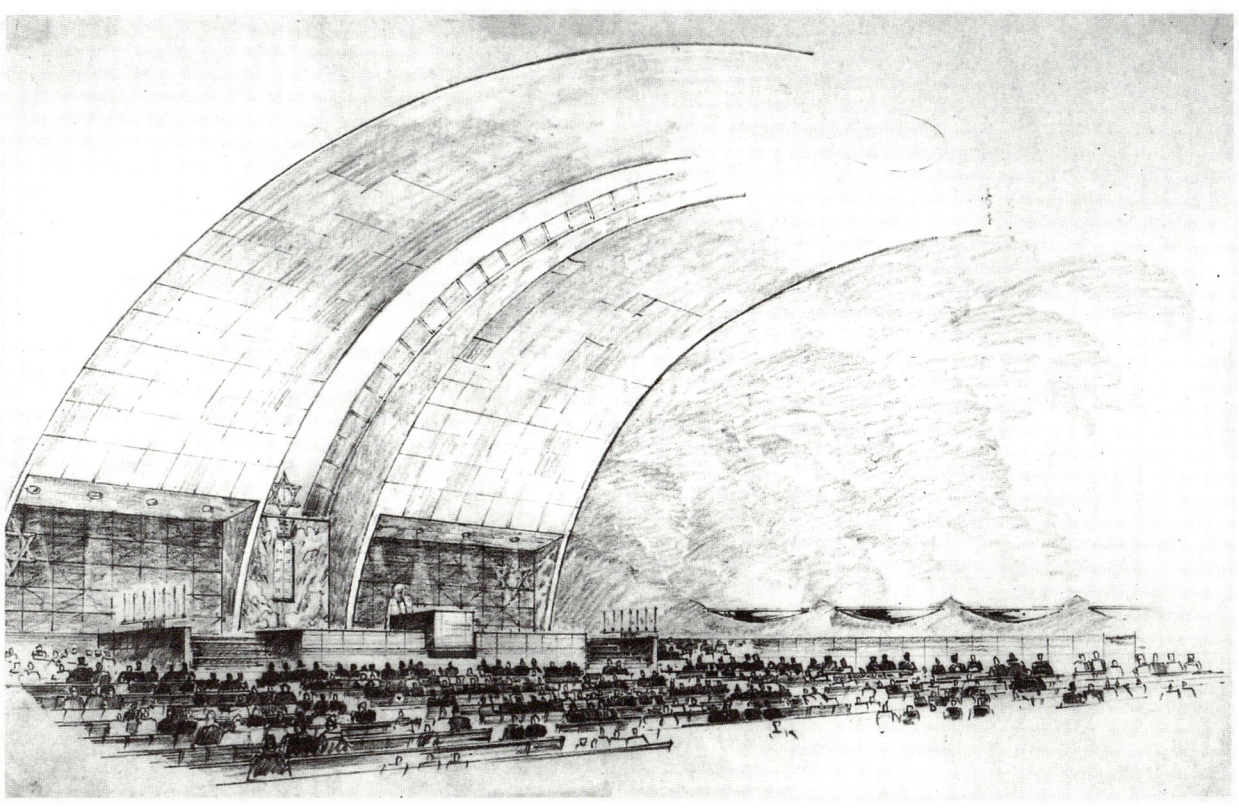

30 Construction of Sanctuary, B'nai Amoona, 1949. Source: B'nai Amoona Archives.

31 Perspective of Sanctuary looking towards Torah Ark, B'nai Amoona, 1946–50. Source: Mendelsohn Archive.

Construction proceeded without much incident, but meanwhile the congregation continued to argue about the new building. The new dispute dealt with seating within the sanctuary. Should men and women be allowed to sit together, as in Reform congregations, or remain apart according to Orthodox custom? At the previous building, the congregation had compromised; on the main floor only a low armrest separated the two halves. Married couples, if they desired, could sit on the right side of this divide, while the more traditional were accommodated by a balcony reserved for women. Now, congregants debated whether or not segregation should be eliminated entirely. For a congregation whose rabbi stressed maintaining the core of Jewish faith and practice, the issue of seating represented a struggle over identity. The minutes of one tumultuous meeting record that "Rabbi Halpern remarked that all innovations do not bring members to the Temple, but if the elimination of segregation would add to the spirituality, he was in favor of the elimination."[80] Eventually, a new compromise was reached that retained a limited amount of segregated seating while allowing the vast majority of the congregants to sit together as families.

By 1949 the congregation had begun to apprehend what they had achieved in commissioning Mendelsohn. Visitors, drawn by a growing number of nationally published accounts of its design, flocked to see the building. Perhaps encouraged by their growing pride in the building, congregants voted in June to spend $100,000 to complete the north wing, although construction of a library and nursery block projecting into the courtyard remained on hold. High Holy Day services were held that fall in the shell of the temple and assembly hall that year. Halpern took special note of the fact that Mendelsohn's synagogue outside Cleveland—whose construction site he visited in November—was costing considerably more than the building nearing completion in University City.[81]

Mendelsohn, too, was pleased. He wrote his wife at the end of June 1950, when he traveled to St. Louis to inspect the nearly completed structure, "The building—still in construction—looks splendid."[82] Three months later, when he returned for the dedication ceremonies, he was satisfied even more with the result. "The building proper is one of my best and very powerful without being heavy," he noted.[83]

The festive dedication ceremonies on September 1–3, 1950, were attended by the congregation and Christian and Jewish religious leaders from throughout the metropolitan area, as well as by Mendelsohn, Bloom, and Millstone. The highlight of the Friday ceremonies was a procession with the Torah scrolls. The following day Kenneth Kranzberg, the son of the congregation's future president, had his bar mitzvah during the first regular service. On Sunday, Rabbi Louis Finkelstein, chancellor of the Jewish Theological Seminary, gave the principal address.

A congregation brochure captured the sense of accomplishment that by now enveloped the building, as the many frustrations that had accompanied its construction began to fade:

> It is indeed a thing of beauty calling attention to all who appreciate the aesthetic and beauty in life. It is the talk of the University, and is subject for discussion in the lecture hall. Architecture students stand in awe and admiration at the courage of our congregation. We can be duly proud of our achievement, even though a part of the original plan had to be postponed. . . . We have stepped away from the traditional style of Synagogue with pillars and domes even though we shall retain the traditions of our fathers in our search for religious inspiration. It is the change that has added so much beauty to our new Shule. It has been our aim to have a House of God that was as attractive physically as it was spiritually. We are convinced that we have succeeded in accomplishing our goal.[84]

House of God; House of the People; House of the Torah

32 Interior, St. Engelbert Church. Source: Pfammatter, Betonkirchen, photo 21.

B'nai Amoona represented a radical departure from the (admittedly increasingly vague) historicist designs that had long dominated American synagogue architecture. Yet, neither Mendelsohn nor the leadership of B'nai Amoona—least of all Rabbi Halpern—conceived of the building as a departure from the core of Jewish beliefs. In the short speech he made at the time of the building's dedication, Mendelsohn declared: "Though at first glance, your new House of Worship might appear to be a decisive break with our people's ancient traditions, a careful study will convince even the most reluctant that this tradition has been maintained in all its principles."[85] Halpern wrote that the new building was "a Mikdash Me-at, a replica, in part, of the ancient Temple in Jerusalem."[86] Such an attitude was possible because throughout Jewish history synagogues had been built in conformance with local architectural traditions.[87] Function, not style, lay at the core of this building type. As powerful as the image of B'nai Amoona's boldly curved girders was, the core of Mendelsohn's achievement lay in accommodating the varied array of spaces necessary to nurture a community of the faithful.

Interviewed in an article published in 1947, Mendelsohn addressed more specifically his approach to the task he faced in University City:

> Today's religious centers should comprise three units: the house of worship, which is the House of God, the assembly hall for adult members, which is the House of the People, the school for the education and recreation of children, which is the House of the Torah. To shelter these three divisions, to bring their different functions into an organic planned relationship, to express their material and mental unification, must be the final aim of the architect."[88]

What were the origins of these ideas and how were they realized at B'nai Amoona?

Mendelsohn's familiarity with recent German church architecture influenced deeply his thinking about religious architecture in general. Bartning and Böhm had stressed the creation of an architecture of community, adding facilities such as assembly halls and classrooms to the basic provision of sacred space. Both had reconceptualized the character of the sacred core of their church complexes by designing spaces intended to bring congregations together as communities united in the shared experience of worship. Both also substituted immaterial light for the historicist ornament that they found too cerebral to capture the emotional power of faith (fig. 32). During the postwar era, the approach came to dominate the design of churches around the world; at B'nai Amoona, Mendelsohn demonstrated that its same principles could be successfully applied to synagogue architecture as well.[89]

Without Bartning and Böhm's emphasis on a modern architectural style, the focus on a community-oriented architecture was already well established in the United States within both the Jewish and Christian communities. Between the wars, Conservative Jewish congregations such as B'nai Amoona had placed great importance upon the provision of school and meeting spaces.[90] After 1945 such an arrangement became even more prevalent, as the synagogue increasingly was the institution charged with promoting a specifically Jewish identity for a community, one poised between the recent destruction of European Jewry in the Holocaust and its own increasing economic success and assimilation. Many Jews who had not attended religious services in the city before migrating to the suburbs now joined congregations to recast their Jewish identity in religious rather than social terms.[91] B'nai Amoona provided the paradigm for the mixture of innovative style and specific functions that would characterize the new suburban synagogue.

Mendelsohn's favorite view of the building showed it in model form (fig. 33).[92] Along with the accompanying plan of the principle level, the model gives a clear idea of his intentions (fig. 34). "The building," he suggested, "as a

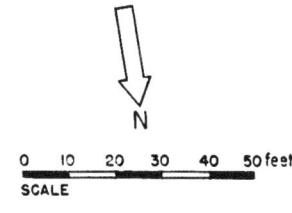

33 Model, B'nai Amoona, 1947. Source: Mendelsohn Archive.

34 Plan, B'nai Amoona, 1947. Source: Mendelsohn Archive.

whole integrates all parts into an architectural organism from which no part can be taken away without destroying the whole—the proof of every artistic achievement."[93] To highlight the quasi-urban character of the site, he filled the blocks to its edges; and whereas many architects would have placed the prominent part of the building front and center, Mendelsohn balanced the site, keeping shapes and heights of the structure also in balance. The most significant example of the latter choice was his location of the temple. It stood on the quietest corner of the site but was easily visible because of its bold profile as seen from the north, the direction from which most people would approach it. The assembly hall buffered the temple in front. Around this block of the building Mendelsohn wrapped the two sides of the school building, from which he projected a library/nursery room into the central court. (The rooms closest to the temple served as a chapel and boardroom.) A small group of offices were nestled across the corridor from the temple and faced out onto the courtyard. A covered breezeway protected the recessed entrance to the building. Fundamental to the composition was Mendelsohn's treatment of the Trinity and Washington corner, a pivotal point where a cantilevered slab roof sitting on a glazed plinth helped anchor the building.

The heart of the building was the temple, entered through the foyer that separated it from the assembly hall. Although the sanctuary of B'nai Amoona was, because of its ritual purpose, the most richly decorated interior Mendelsohn had yet designed, light and space dominated its ornamental details. Mendelsohn was pleased with the results:

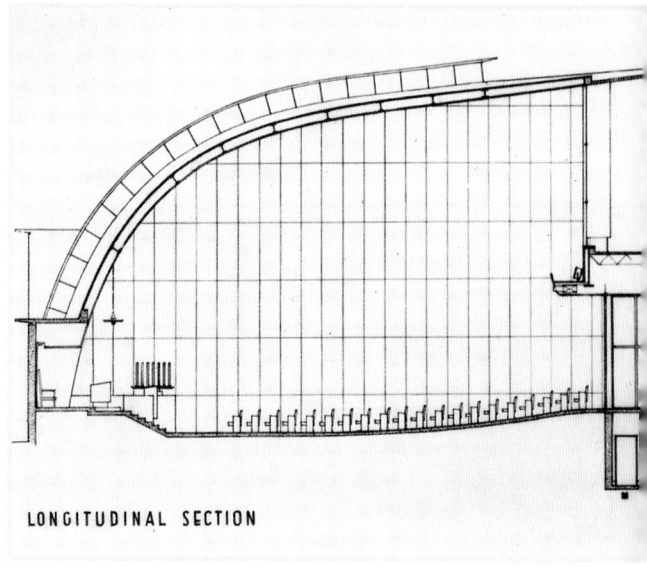

35 Longitudinal Section, B'nai Amoona, 1947–50. Source: Mendelsohn Archive.

The inside exactly as I envisioned it, light—day and night—perfect, the cream-white colored chair fabric matching the curved ceiling and the dark-brown chair structure matching the podium. The ark magnificent. A piece of Art and very well executed. Its perforated tender design and material—silver bronze and brass—in contrast to the serene structural lines of the shell.[94]

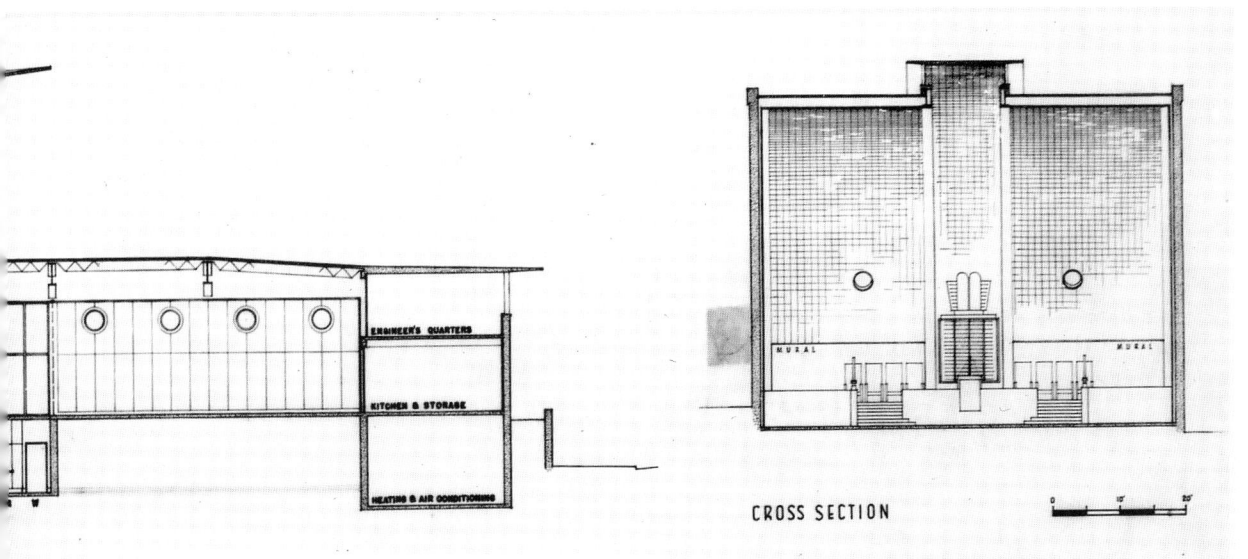

36 Sanctuary, B'nai Amoona. Source: B'nai Amoona.

At one end of the temple, a clerestory window, shaded slightly by fin mullions, let daylight into the space, whose length was also marked in the center by a light trough raised above the ceiling that curved downwards towards its east end (fig. 35). Together, these windows ensured that light would accent the sacred furnishings mounted on the dais (fig. 36). Anchored at each end by identical candelabra, this platform contained at its center first the bima, or pulpit, above which hung the sacred flame and behind which stood the most important object of all, the ark. Holder of the Torah scrolls and crowned with the tablets of the law—inscribed in Hebrew with the Ten Commandments— the ark was the most important object in the building and one of the most decorative Mendelsohn ever designed (fig. 37).

Key to Mendelsohn's thinking about the synagogue plan was the flexibility he enabled with the sanctuary space, which could be expanded to accommodate the crowds that came

37

38

37　Torah Shrine, B'nai Amoona. Source: Mendelsohn Archive.

38　Sanctuary open to assembly hall for High Holy Day services, B'nai Amoona. Source: B'nai Amoona.

39　Ferer Assembly Hall, B'nai Amoona, Purim, 1954. Source: B'nai Amoona Archives.

each fall to attend services on the two holiest days of the Jewish year, Rosh Hashanah and Yom Kippur. At B'nai Amoona, collapsible partition walls could be folded back to allow the Morris and Lottie Spitzer Chapel, the boardroom beyond it, and the Ferer Assembly Hall to be incorporated into the sanctuary space (fig. 38). Mendelsohn provided additional seating in the basement recreation room (fig. 39). Altogether, sixteen hundred people could be accommodated, although the sanctuary itself sat only 674.[95] Mendelsohn took special care with the design of the assembly hall. Notations on several drawings show him calculating how many people it could seat on various occasions, ranging from banquets to concerts.[96] The assembly hall was intended to serve the congregation's adult members as the community's secular heart, encouraging their identification with and as Jews at a time of increasing assimilation.

Equally crucial to the synagogue's mission was the education of its children as Jews. Although most of the congregation's children attended public schools,

secular education was supplemented by a rigorous instructional program in Hebrew, Jewish history, and religion, and by extensive recreational programs, many of which encouraged identification with the fate of a newly independent Israel. Each of Mendelsohn's synagogues had a substantial classroom wing. At B'nai Amoona, two sides of the courtyard banked a corridor, off of which opened seven classrooms on the main floor and an additional four upstairs. The porthole windows along this corridor, which echo the form of the door handles to the classrooms, are one of the finest architectural notes animating otherwise entirely utilitarian spaces. Ample natural lighting played a crucial role, too, allowing Mendelsohn to create an entirely glazed north wall. This wall spoke of the openness of the kind of architecture he had designed for thirty years, which was still new for this place and purpose.

Mendelsohn's careful attention to program did not account alone for the building's success, much less its importance. Style did matter. In adopting an obviously contemporary visage for their synagogue, the members of B'nai Amoona proved prescient. Across the United States, postwar Jews would turn to modernism to distance themselves from the exotic connotations of earlier Islamicist, Byzantine, and Romanesque synagogue architecture. Successful suburban Jews now wanted to be part of the American mainstream, which they helped lead towards a more inclusive architecture oriented in the present rather than the past. Moreover, references to Middle Eastern origins seemed inappropriate now that Israeli Jews had won their independence in a war against their Arab neighbors. (Nor did it hurt the cause of modern architecture among American Jews that the British Mandate of Palestine had been one of the first places the style had flourished.) In turning to Mendelsohn, the University City congregation had demonstrated a courage whose purpose was not to shock or startle but to maintain an ancient faith.

A Place in History?

B'nai Amoona quickly was published in the local and the national popular press and featured in architecture magazines in the United States and Europe. In the understanding of the Jewish and the architectural communities, B'nai Amoona, along with Mendelsohn's subsequent synagogue designs, had established the paradigm for the postwar development of this building type, at least in the United States. Its success encouraged the construction of modern churches as well as synagogues in the St. Louis area and anticipated the emphasis architects working in the region would soon place on dramatic, curved spans. Nonetheless, neither B'nai Amoona nor any of Mendelsohn's other buildings became icons of postwar American architecture to the degree of such works as Mies van der Rohe's Lake Shore Drive Apartments in Chicago or Eero Saarinen's General Motors Technical Center in Warren, Michigan. Even the Harvard Graduate Center in Cambridge, Massachusetts, designed by Gropius's new firm, The Architects' Collaborative, although devoid of the exquisite detailing and the deftly balanced asymmetry of the architect's earlier Bauhaus, is far better known to students of modern architecture than any of the buildings Mendelsohn designed after leaving Germany. Also more prominent are the postwar synagogues of a trio of gentile architects: Gropius, Philip Johnson, and Wright. Why was B'nai Amoona's success and that of its architect so circumscribed?

Although its building was not included quickly in histories of American architecture, the congregation of B'nai Amoona had plenty of reasons to be satisfied, not only with the way it functioned, but also with the favorable attention it garnered. Location more than design probably accounted for the rapid growth of the membership in the years just after the move to University City. Even before Mendelsohn was commissioned, 230 new families joined B'nai Amoona after the purchase of the University City site; the congregation doubled again in size—to more than one thousand members—in the decade following the building's dedication.[97] Although the fact that B'nai Amoona was the first non-Reform synagogue located so far west probably accounted for almost all of this growth, the publication of the building in the color Sunday supplement of the *Post-Dispatch* in December 1950 certainly did not hurt.[98] From the supplement, potential members of the congregation and their neighbors learned that the building was "simple yet dramatic in appearance" and that it represented "an expression of the ability of Eric Mendelsohn, internationally renowned architect, to relate form and function dynamically."[99]

Residents of University City and the region could also observe throughout the fifties the impact of Mendelsohn's approach to religious architecture on local architects, many of whom had likely noticed the synagogue's repeated publication in the nation's most

40 Shaare Zedek Synagogue, University City, Bernard Bloom, 1950 and 1956. Source: Missouri Historical Society.

41 Faith-Salem Evangelical and Reformed Congregation, Jennings, Missouri, Frederick Dunn, 1951.

esteemed architectural magazine, *Architectural Forum*, whose April 1953 cover it graced.[100] When Orthodox congregations moved into University City in the early fifties, the architects they hired invoked Mendelsohn's curvilinear modern vocabulary without repeating his expensive engineering. Bloom could of course draw upon direct experience with Mendelsohn when he designed Shaare Zedek, while Ben Shapiro revealed an equally careful study of B'nai Amoona in his nearby building for Chesed Shel Emeth, dedicated in 1951 (fig. 40).[101] B'nai Amoona clearly influenced Frederick Dunn's ability to design a modern building for Faith-Salem Evangelical and Reformed Congregation, completed in 1951 (fig. 41). To encourage them to accept a modern design, Dunn took members of Faith-Salem to see new religious structures in the area. "The climax of the tour came," he acknowledged, "when the committee reached the new modernist B'nai Amoona Synagogue in University City. This fine building really bowled our committee over."[102]

42

The most acclaimed religious structure erected in St. Louis during the fifties did not have such a direct connection to B'nai Amoona, but the two could nonetheless be paired in several ways. The Resurrection of Our Lord Roman Catholic Church in south St. Louis—designed by Joseph Murphy and Eugene Mackey—was dedicated in 1954 (figs. 42 and 43). A newspaper article on the region's new religious architecture noted that the building was "considered by many students of architecture to be one of the finest modern churches in America."[103] Published along with B'nai Amoona in the French architecture journal *L'architecture d'aujourd'hui* in 1957, this building embodied the ideals of the liturgical movement launched in Germany during the twenties.[104] The dedication program emphasized how the shape of the space was intended to impact congregants:

The parabola, graceful and symbolic, connotes an open-armed, general welcome. Someone has said that the church seems to enfold the worshipper and the visitor and to lead each unerringly to the heart and focal point, the altar.[105]

42 Resurrection of Our Lord Roman Catholic Church, St. Louis, Murphy and Mackey, 1954. Source: Missouri Historical Society.

43 Interior, Resurrection of Our Lord Roman Catholic Church. Source: Missouri Historical Society.

Murphy identified some of the more pragmatic reasons for the popularity of such abstract architectural form:

"Today there is almost no parish or congregation that can afford the labor, craftsmanship or materials required to erect the massive structures of the past. The ideas and faiths of the great religions have not changed, but present economic conditions make it impossible to carry them out architecturally in the way of our forefathers. Besides, we have new standards of comfort and convenience and new methods of achieving them. Modern church architecture tries to meet these practical requirements and at the same time reflect the deep values of our religion and culture."[106]

Mendelsohn himself never would have offered such a mundane defense of what he viewed as an issue primarily of artistic expression of the reality of a changing world, but the high price of labor surely helped send his clients in the direction of modern architecture. While churches continued to be built in a variety of styles, postwar synagogues became showpieces of the modern movement. From the beginning, commentators recognized B'nai Amoona and Mendelsohn's subsequent synagogue designs as the progenitors of this development. As early as 1947, before ground had even been broken in University City, the architectural historian Rachel Wischnitzer-Bernstein, writing in *Commentary*, concluded an article titled

44 Park Synagogue, Cleveland Heights, Ohio, Mendelsohn, 1945–50. Source: Mendelsohn Archive.

"The Problem of Synagogue Architecture: Creating a Style Expressive of America" with a plea that Mendelsohn and others like him be given the opportunity to create alternatives to historical styles. After noting that B'nai Amoona would be set into an environment that included a number of "period pieces," she concluded, "Granted the necessity for tact, Mr. Mendelsohn will still have to make some bold departures; and it is precisely here that he will need the understanding and cooperation of the Jewish community. What Mr. Mendelsohn produces may supply at least a partial indication of the future of American synagogue architecture."[107]

Wischnitzer-Bernstein's prophecy was quickly fulfilled, as Mendelsohn received commissions for additional synagogues in Cleveland Heights, Ohio; Grand Rapids, Michigan; and St. Paul, Minnesota, while designs for buildings in Baltimore, Washington, D.C., and Dallas made it to the planning stages (and beyond in the case of Baltimore, where the school wing was built).[108] Of these, the Park Synagogue in Cleveland Heights was the earliest and one of the most ambitious (fig. 44). In November 1945 Mendelsohn made plans to travel from St. Louis to Cleveland to be interviewed by a congregation that reportedly was ready to spend $500,000.[109] Like B'nai Amoona, Park Synagogue purchased their suburban property in 1942 and dedicated their building eight years later. Here, too, Mendelsohn had to thoroughly revise his initial design after bids came three times over budget, and a school wing was completed only several years later. The basic program of the two synagogues was similar, with a sanctuary expandable on High Holy Days into the foyer and an assembly hall supplemented by classrooms, offices, and a library.[110] Just as Mendelsohn in the 1920s had designed individual Schocken stores in Nuremberg, Stuttgart, and Chemnitz, so now, in the last years of his life, did he fashion entirely unique structures for each congregation that approached him. A St. Louis reporter summarized Mendelsohn's remarks, delivered in 1950 in a lecture at Washington University attended by 500 architects, professors, and students:

> Eric Mendelsohn . . . said here yesterday that the United States is the most important architectural center of the world but that unadorned functionalism is having a devastating effect on young architects. . . . Mendelsohn stressed that he had himself been drawn to the prophets of functionalism but pointed out, by means of slides, that he had combined a regard with function with sensitivity to form for its own sake.[111]

In Cleveland Heights, Mendelsohn realized a circular sanctuary, such as the one he had initially intended to build for B'nai Amoona. Here, he also demonstrated what he could have achieved on the more ample sites considered and rejected by the University City congregation. The result was a building that accommodated almost exactly the same program as its Missouri counterpart, but in a way uniquely appropriate for its location.

This lack of interest in standardization was one of the things that separated Mendelsohn from the two most celebrated of German emigré architects, Mies and Gropius. A January 1950 visit to Chicago gave Mendelsohn the opportunity to assess the recent work of his longtime rival.[112] Mies courteously escorted him around the campus he had designed for the Illinois Institute of Technology, whose architecture program he directed. Mendelsohn wrote his wife, "He [has] found his formula and intends apparently to stand on it until the end, square and academic, . . . a rigid synthesis of principles which will kill (quickly as well as painless) the new hope of a free humanity."[113] He was equally scathing about Mies's colleague Ludwig Hilbersheimer, whom he labeled "a dried up onion."[114]

Mendelsohn's American circle differed significantly from the one nurtured by the Museum of Modern Art's Department of Architecture and Design, which helped bring both Mies and Gropius to the United States and continued to publicize them for years. The architects and critics he found he could depend on were engaged in the task of creating a modern architecture which, while deeply indebted to the International Style developed in Europe during the twenties, was less industrial and less divorced from nature. Taking Wright's deft siting and use of materials as their point of departure, they favored an architecture more deeply rooted in specifically American concerns, such as the single family suburban house.[115] Mendelsohn's identification with this approach, usually labeled regional although it pervaded the entire country, is clear from the list of references he provided while campaigning for an appointment to the faculty of

Washington University and by his move in 1945 to San Francisco, where it had flourished for more than a decade. The supporters he named included Talbot Hamlin, of the Avery Library at Columbia, a prominent historian and critic of American architecture; William Wurster, then the dean of architecture at MIT, a position he would later assume at the University of California, Berkeley; Lewis Mumford, the distinguished architectural and cultural critic; and George Howe, the Philadelphia architect who with William Lescaze had designed PSFS, a Philadelphia skyscraper whose details owed much to Mendelsohn's Schocken stores.[116] Wurster was at that time the most prominent architect of his generation.

The shift towards a more naturalized modernism was not strictly American, although European-oriented opposition often labeled its American proponents provincial. Wurster brought Alvar Aalto, one of the new style's most prominent European advocates, to MIT to teach and to build Baker hall, a student dormitory. Even Le Corbusier turned away from a machine-based aesthetic during the 1930s, while already in the twenties Böhm provided a precedent for an architecture that cloaked new sculptural forms in traditional materials and purposes. Nonetheless, in the United States by 1950 a divide had opened up between the mostly native-born architects who supported this new trend and the many emigrés and their students who espoused greater austerity and closer ties to CIAM ("Congrés Internationaux d'Architecture Moderne" or International Congress of Modern Architecture), an international organization of modern architects. The gap had not been so pronounced when Mendelsohn arrived in New York in 1941. Even the curatorial staff of the Museum of Modern Art was temporarily supportive.[117] For Mendelsohn, becoming an American involved attaching himself to a position that he recognized as instrumental to his adopted land's acceptance of new architectural forms. This effort entailed everything from collecting photographs of colonial and antebellum domestic architecture to seeing Wright rather than Mies as his most important model and rival.[118]

Mendelsohn's admiration for Wurster and other architects such as Harwell Hamilton Harris, who practiced in Northern California, influenced his design of a house for the Winston family. This project, for a site in Clayton, Missouri, is characteristic of the modest houses, sheathed in wood, erected just before and after the war in the hills of the Bay Area, many of them designed by Mendelsohn's erstwhile partners, Dinwiddie and Hill. Two tiers of cantilevered roofs perched lightly atop ribbon windows. The result is informal and open. The house was never built, largely because the skeletal steel frame construction Mendelsohn proposed proved too expensive.[119] The error was typical of those made by emigrés unfamiliar with the gap between the seductive image of the naked frames of half-completed skyscrapers and the prosaic reality of inexpensive domestic construction in wood.

One reason for the increasing marginalization of such designs was their association with the increasingly eccentric Frank Lloyd Wright, whom by the fifties, despite the enthusiastic reception of the Guggenheim Museum, was more often identified with the past than the present. Wright was nevertheless the American whose architecture Mendelsohn most admired and who defined for him the character of America's built environment. His admiration was not unbounded, however. In the late forties, the two men competed for the chance to build a synagogue for a congregation in Washington, D.C. The rabbi's wife was related to the Pittsburgh Kaufmanns, Wright's clients for Falling Water. Mendelsohn commented, "[Wright's] performance some weeks ago before the committee was most amazing and—as the Rabbi saw—bewildering. He apparently has offered to do the work for nearly nothing. Seems as if he would like to have his work in the Capital [sic] before he goes to Walhalla."[120] According to Mendelsohn, Wright became "mystical" when he saw the site, while Mendelsohn remained "rational."[121] Later, when it appeared that he had won the commission (in fact, neither man was to build it), he became more snide:

The well-bred Rabbi and his Kaufmann Pittsburgh wife have given up on the Azher king, and seem set on Eric Mendelsohn. The King's performance before the committee—some months ago—was arrogant and out to teach my Jews how to build their house of worship. Didn't work.[122]

What Wright and Mendelsohn shared in these years, in sharp distinction from Mies, Gropius, and even Neutra, was a sense of form as something plastic. Although Mendelsohn failed to place himself in the acknowledged forefront of contemporary American architecture, his more sculptural approach certainly became one of the hallmarks of many of the most exciting new American buildings of the fifties and early sixties. Nowhere was this truer than in St. Louis. The young Eero Saarinen probably had not thought of Mendelsohn's B'nai Amoona design, recently published in *Architectural Forum*, when in 1948 he designed his competition entry for the city's Gateway Arch (fig. 45). Completed in 1965, Saarinen's stunning design became the emblem of the postwar city. Although Mendelsohn never combined such feats of engineering with such simplicity and indeed never built on the scale of the 630-foot-high monument, Saarinen was certainly an admirer of the older architect's sketches, which strongly influenced the design of his Dulles Airport outside Washington, D.C.[123]

St. Louis's own new airport, Lambert Field, offers another example of the realization in the 1950s of the kind of forms Mendelsohn had dreamed of building four decades earlier. Here, Minoru Yamasaki designed a sequence of intersecting, thin-shell concrete vaults that captured the

45 Gateway Arch, Jefferson National Expansion Monument, Eero Saarinen, 1948–65, St. Louis. Source: Missouri Historical Society.

lightness of flight and of state-of-the-art construction (fig. 46). Gyo Obata—of the St. Louis firm Hellmuth, Obata + Kassabaum—assisted by the Italian engineer Pier Luigi Nervi, demonstrated that such vaults could be marvelously decorative in his Priory Chapel, completed in St. Louis County in 1962 (fig. 47).[124] Although Obata may not have been aware of the fact, Mendelsohn had used similar vaults—though not arranged around a central space—in his unbuilt design for Beth El Synagogue in Baltimore (fig. 48).

The divides in postwar American architectural culture that separated old from young, native- from foreign-born, adherents of curved from proponents of straight lines did little to hinder the widespread adoption of modern architecture by institutional and commercial clients. Universities, governments, and corporations appreciated its efficient and—in comparison to the lavishly decorated architecture of the twenties—inexpensive construction. At a time when American society was becoming more homogeneous, economically and socially, the no longer startling abstraction offered by what was still perceived as a new architecture remained refreshingly independent of traditional marks of class and status. Few were as persistent in their adoption of modern architecture and in their pursuit of artistic excellence as the building committees of the country's new largely suburban synagogues.

The Jewish community took pride in the placement of Mendelsohn's synagogues in publications that focused on their architecture.[125] Nonetheless, congregations across the country did not hesitate to hire gentile architects if it would ensure that they received a distinguished building. Among the most notable of the new synagogues were Gropius and The Architects' Collaborative's Oheb Shalom Temple in Baltimore of 1957; Philip Johnson's Kneses Tifereth in Port Chester, New York, of 1954–56; and Wright's Beth Shalom in Elkins Park, Pennsylvania, of 1953–59 (figs. 49–51). In each case, as in Mendelsohn's synagogues,

46 Lambert International Airport, Hellmuth, Yamasaki, and Leinweber, St. Louis, 1957. Source: Missouri Historical Society.

47 Priory Chapel, Hellmuth, Obata + Kassabaum with Pier Luigi Nervi, St. Louis County, 1962. Source: Missouri Historical Society.

48 Perspective, Beth El Synagogue, Mendelsohn, Baltimore, Maryland, 1948. Source: Whittick, Mendelsohn, fig. 98b.

49

49 Oheb Shalom Synagogue,
The Architects' Collaborative,
Baltimore, 1957.
Source: *Architectural Record* 135
(June 1964): 147.

50 Kneses Tifereth Synagogue,
Philip Johnson, Port Chester,
New York, 1954–56.
Source: *L'architecture d'aújourd'hui*
28 (April–May 1957): 79.

51 Beth Shalom Synagogue,
Frank Lloyd Wright, Elkins Park,
Pennsylvania, 1953–59.
Source: *Architettura: Cronache e storia*
8 (June 1963): 95.

the shape of the sanctuary and the way it was illuminated drove the design rather than historicist references.

Although Christian congregations in the United States were reluctant on the whole to engage in such experimentalism, the widespread acceptance of modern architecture around the world during the 1950s ensured that its adherents increasingly would be called upon to make the transition from representing the "spirit of the age" to capturing a sense of the eternal in their designs for churches as well as synagogues. Early examples of American churches built in the spirit of Bartning's and Böhm's reforms include Eliel and Eero Saarinen's Tabernacle Church of Christ in Columbus, Indiana, of 1940–42, and their Christ Lutheran Church in Minneapolis, Minnesota, completed in 1950 (fig. 52). Elsewhere, Oscar Niemeyer's church dedicated to St. Francis of Assisi in Pampulha, Brazil, of 1946 and Le Corbusier's pilgrimage church of Ronchamp, France, of 1950–54 numbered the most celebrated buildings of their day (figs. 53 and 54).

Why was Mendelsohn so seldom acknowledged as a participant in these international developments? Most significantly, he remained at a slight distance from the people and institutions who set architectural fashions. Even in Germany, as a Jew who specialized in commercial architecture, Mendelsohn had been something of an outsider among fellow avant-garde architects. In the United States, where he immigrated in middle age, this proved even truer. Although widely respected and frequently published, he remained something of an anomaly, detached from the centers of opinion-making and fashion. Almost as significant in these years was his focus—although he seldom attended religious services—upon nurturing the faith he had been raised in, a faith he had seen all but exterminated in his native land. In America his architectural ambition was almost entirely confined to designs that served the Jewish community. At a time when style rather than function was paramount in architectural criticism, his function-oriented approach did little to promote him among other architects or the general public. None of these challenges hindered his ability to achieve the task he set himself at B'nai Amoona: to create a synagogue architecture that would sustain Judaism in an American present, where it belonged as completely as it had to past European or Middle Eastern contexts.

52

52 Christ Lutheran Church,
Eliel and Eero Saarinen, Minneapolis,
Minnesota, 1949–50.
Source: *Architectural Forum* 93
(July 1950): 85.

53 San Francesco d'Assisi,
Oscar Niemeyer, Pampulha,
Brazil, 1946. Source: Joseph Picard,
Modern Church Architecture
(New York: Orion Press, 1960), 171.

54 Notre Dame, Le Corbusier, Ronchamp, France, 1950–54. Source: Le Corbusier, *Oeuvre Complète, 1952–57* (Zurich: Grisberger, W. Boesiger, 1957), 19.

Epilogue

B'nai Amoona continued for many years to flourish in its new building. Initially, the new building entailed only one small deviation from Mendelsohn's design. The $130,000 wing completed in 1957 by Bernard Bloom, Mendelsohn's local collaborator, housed offices instead of the library and nursery anticipated by Mendelsohn and also featured five additional classrooms. Because of this shift in function, Bloom built it off the existing offices, from which it extended into the courtyard rather than off the classrooms to the north.[126] By the 1970s, however, the viability of the synagogue's location at the eastern end of University City was called into question. Just as more prescient members of the congregation had realized in the 1940s, most of B'nai Amoona's members now lived far to the west. Following the lead of the many synagogues that had already abandoned the city of St. Louis—now entirely devoid of Jewish houses of worship—as well as its innermost suburbs, B'nai Amoona began once again to move farther west. The congregation responded initially by erecting a single-story building on South Mason Road deep in St. Louis County that housed the offices, classrooms, assembly hall, and recreational facilities. Finally, congregants decided to move their religious services to the new site as well.

Realizing the importance of architecture, they chose one of St. Louis's most prominent architects, Gyo Obata, to design their new home (eventually completed in 1986). Sensitive to his clients' pride in their distinguished history, Obata integrated stained-glass windows from the Academy and Vernon Synagogue as well as Mendelsohn's Tabernacle Shrine into his design (fig. 55).

B'nai Amoona's departure from the home designed for it by Mendelsohn raised questions about the fate of a cherished local landmark.[127] Luckily, the same qualities that Mendelsohn sought to imbue into his synagogue proved to have secular applications as well. B'nai Amoona became one of a number of local synagogues to be converted into a cultural institution. In 1986 Richard Baron, a local developer, spearheaded the transformation of the building into the Center of Contemporary Arts.[128] Executed by Trivers Architects, the architectural changes were relatively minor. After receiving a new floor, the assembly hall became a dance studio (fig. 56). The addition of a stage and blackout paint turned the sanctuary into a theater. The chapel became a green room. Elsewhere, the original classrooms, recreation areas, and offices continue to function as Mendelsohn had intended. Most of Bloom's addition now serves as a gallery. The result is a building that continues to encourage a sense of community, albeit one now predicated upon dance, music, and the visual arts.

55 Interior, B'nai Amoona Synagogue,
Hellmuth, Obata + Kassabaum,
St. Louis County, 1986.
Source: Missouri Historical Society.

56 Dance studio, COCA. Source: COCA.

Fifty years after its dedication, Mendelsohn's building retains its vitality, although the shock of the new has long since worn off. Its orange brick walls still serve to integrate it into the neighborhood—on whose institutional edge it sits—even as the parabolic profile of the roofline still distinguishes it from the surrounding largely Georgian houses. A Star of David on the exterior of the sanctuary wall honors its original function. Most importantly, the interior remains full of people of varied backgrounds and all ages pursuing their particular interests with passion and dedication. Although no longer a House of God or the Torah, it remains, as Mendelsohn intended from the beginning, very much a House of the People.

Notes

1. *B'nai Amoona Sixtieth Jubilee, 1882–1942* (St. Louis, 1942). A copy of this volume can be found in the St. Louis Jewish Community Archives, Saul Brodsky Library, St. Louis County, Missouri.

2. "Dedication Ceremony Attended by 1400," *St. Louis Globe-Democrat*, 14 January 1932.

3. Gerald Gamm, *Urban Exodus: Why the Jews Left Boston and the Catholics Stayed* (Cambridge: Harvard University Press, 1999), 24–29, on the importance of prewar suburbanization in relation to Jewish migration within and beyond Boston.

4. Sandy Spitzer, Interview with the author, May 1999. Spitzer's father, S. Barney Spitzer, was president of the congregation throughout the 1940s.

5. In 1946, following his receipt of American citizenship, Mendelsohn anglicized the spelling of his first name, dropping the final "h."

6. For an overview of Mendelsohn's career, see Regina Stephan, ed., *Erich Mendelsohn: Gebaute Welten* (Stuttgart: Hatje Verlag, 1998).

7. Eric Mendelsohn, "In the Spirit of Our Age," *Commentary* 3 (1947): 541.

8. Bruno Zevi, *Erich Mendelsohn: The Complete Works* (Basel: Birkhäuser Verlag, 1999), 6, 122–23, 128–29; and Kathleen James, "Kleinere Bauten für die jüdische Gemeinschaft in Tilsit, Königsberg und Essen," in Stephan, *Mendelsohn*, 167–77.

9. Rosalind M. Bronson, *B'nai Amoona for All Generations* (University City: Congregation B'nai Amoona, 1982), 1–111.

10. Bronson, *B'nai Amoona*, 112.

11. B'nai Amoona follows almost exactly the model described in David Kaufman, *Shul with a Pool: The "Synagogue Center" in American Jewish History* (Hanover: Brandeis University Press, 1999).

12. The mobility of synagogues and their congregants is stressed throughout Gamm, *Urban Exodus*.

13. Bronson, *B'nai Amoona*, 20–23, 76.

14. Kaufman, *Shul with a Pool*, 180.

15. Brian de Breffny, *The Synagogue* (New York: Macmillan, 1978), 156–90.

16. Bronson, *B'nai Amoona*, 97–118.

17. Bronson, *B'nai Amoona*, 141–44.

18. Abraham Halpern, "Our Congregation," *B'nai Amoona Sixtieth Jubilee*.

19. "Spirit of 1942," *B'nai Amoona Sixtieth Jubilee*. Spitzer, the president of the congregation, was an ardent Zionist, as was Halpern. Kranzberg, who succeeded Spitzer in 1950, and Ferer, who chaired the building committee, remained skeptical at this time. Sandy Spitzer, Ken Kranzberg, and Jackie Guttmann, interviews with the author, May 1999.

20. Albert Einstein, "Humanity on Trial," *B'nai Amoona Sixtieth Jubilee*.

21. Abram L. Sachar, *B'nai Amoona Sixtieth Jubilee*.

22. Israel Goldstein, "American Jewry Comes of Age," *B'nai Amoona Sixtieth Jubilee*.

23. Peter Winston, interview with the author, June 1998. See also Frank Peters, "A Great Architect's Vision As It Rose in St. Louis," *St. Louis Post-Dispatch*, 11 September 1983, 5C.

24. Kathleen James, *Erich Mendelsohn and the Architecture of German Modernism* (Cambridge: Cambridge University Press, 1997), 102–7.

25. Peter Winston, interview with the author, June 1998.

26. Louise Mendelsohn, "The last creative season," in Zevi, *Complete Works*, 276.

27. Eric Mendelsohn, *Three Lectures on Architecture* (Berkeley: University of California Press, 1944).

28. Gilbert Harris to Charles Nagel, letter of 24 December, 1943, The St. Louis Art Museum Archives, St. Louis, Missouri; and Erich Mendelsohn to Victor Packman, letter of 17 November 1943, Mendelsohn Archives, Kunstbibliothek, Staatliche Preußischer Kulturbesitz, Berlin, Germany.

29. Walter E. Orthwein, "St. Mark's Episcopal Started New Trend 25 Years Ago," *St. Louis Globe-Democrat*, 11–12 January 1964.

30. Copies of the checklist for the exhibit as displayed in Chicago survive in the Archives of the St. Louis Art Museum and the Chicago Arts Club.

31. "Architecture of Eric Mendelsohn, 1914–40," typescript with handwritten amendations by Eric Mendelsohn, Archives, St. Louis Art Museum.

32. Hans Rudolf Morganthaler, *The Early Sketches of German Architect Erich Mendelsohn (1887–1953): No Compromise with Reality* (Lewiston: Edwin Mellen Press, 1992).

33. The standard work on Mendelsohn's years in Mandate Palestine is Ita Heinze-Mühleib, *Erich Mendelsohn, Bauten und Projekte in Palästina, 1934–41* (Munich: Scaneg, 1986). See also Ita Heinze-Greenberg, "Bauten in Palästina 1934 bis 1941," in Stephan, *Mendelsohn*, 266–75, and Alona Nitzan-Shiftan, "Contested Zionism—Alternative Modernism. Eric Mendelsohn and the Tel Aviv Chug in Mandate Palestine," *Architectural History* 39 (1996): 147–80.

34. Elodie Courter to William Eisendrath, letter of 4 November 1941, Art Club Archives, Newberry Library, Chicago, Illinois. I thank Wolfgang Voigt for supplying me with this reference.

35. "Architecture of Eric Mendelsohn," press release, Archives, St. Louis Art Museum.

36. Clipping dated 8 March 1944, Mendelsohn File, Fine Arts Department, St. Louis Public Library.

37. H. R. B., "Mendelsohn Exhibition Is Well Worth Visiting," *Globe-Democrat*, 9 March 1944, Archives, St. Louis Art Museum. The house for the man who would become the first president of Israel and his wife was built in Rehovat between 1934 and 1936.

38. "Noted Architect's Work on Exhibit," clipping dated 9 March 1944, Fine Arts Department, St. Louis Public Library.

39. Eric to Louise Mendelsohn, letter of 16 March 1944, Mendelsohn Archive.

40. Mendelsohn to Packman, letter of 21 June 1944, Mendelsohn Archive.

41. Ibid.

42. Barney Spitzer, "To the Officers and Members," 23 October, 1945, B'nai Amoona Archives, Town and Country, Missouri, for the hope that the congregation could be in its new building by the fall of 1947.

43. "Our Dream Comes True. . . ," undated brochure, B'nai Amoona Archives.

44. Eric to Louise Mendelsohn, letter of 6 March 1946, Mendelsohn Archive.

45. Eric to Louise Mendelsohn, letter of 21 October 1945, Mendelsohn Archive.

46. Eric to Louise Mendelsohn, letters of 9, 11 November 1945, Mendelsohn Archive.

47. Minutes, meeting of the entire membership, 19 December 1945, B'nai Amoona Archives.

48. Richard Biedrzynski, *Kirchen Unserer Zeit* (München: Hirmer Verlag, 1958), 35.

49. *Dominikus Böhm*, introduction by Cardinal Joseph Frings, with essays by August Hoff, Herbert Muck, and Raimund Thoma (München: Verlag Schnell & Steiner, 1962), 14.

50. Otto Bartning, *Vom neuen Kirchbau* (Berlin: Bruno Cassirer Verlag, 1919).

51. This is clear from the notations on the drawing published in Zevi, *Complete Works*, 301, fig. 13, where these notes are illegible.

52. I identify the drawing in Zevi, *Complete Works*, 300, figs. 1–7, 9; 301, figs. 10–14, 304; fig. 6 with this first version of the design. Note that Zevi published the drawing on 300, fig. 5 upside down.

53. Other drawings illustrating this design are found in Zevi, *Complete Works*, 303; fig. 3; 304, fig. 4.

54. See also Zevi, *Complete Works*, 301, fig. 15; 303, figs. 1, 4; 304, figs. 1 (Zevi reverses this image), 3, 7.

55. See also Zevi, *Complete Works*, 305, figs. 10–12.

56. See also Zevi, *Complete Works*, 303, fig. 6; 304, fig. 5.

57. For an alternative account, see Hans Morganthaler, "Arbeiten in den USA," in Stephan, *Mendelsohn*, 289–92.

58. Eric Mendelsohn, remarks at the dedication of B'nai Amoona, quoted in Bronson, *B'nai Amoona*, 151.

59. Eric to Louise Mendelsohn, letter of 2 March 1946, Mendelsohn Archive, and Minutes, 4 March 1946, B'nai Amoona Archives.

60. Eric to Louise Mendelsohn, letter of 6 March 1946, Mendelsohn Archive.

61. Ibid.

62. This information is drawn from the plan drawings in the Mendelsohn Archive.

63. Plan drawing 4105, Mendelsohn Archive. Other drawings from this set have both May and June dates from 1946.

64. Eric to Louise Mendelsohn, letter of 21 June 1946, Mendelsohn Archive.

65. Bronson, *B'nai Amoona*, 147.

66. Bronson, *B'nai Amoona*, 151–56.

67. Eric to Louise Mendelsohn, letter of 3 May 1947, was written from St. Louis.

68. There is no record in the Mendelsohn Archive of either set of plans, which were probably never fully drafted.

69. Minutes, 13 October, 4 November, 1 December 1947, and 5 January 1948, B'nai Amoona Archives.

70. Bronson, *B'nai Amoona*, 145.

71. Bronson, *B'nai Amoona*, 148.

72. "B'nai Amoona to Break Ground," *The Jewish Post*, Missouri edition, 10 September 1948.

73. "Groundbreaking for an Unusual Edifice," *St. Louis Post-Dispatch*, 12 September 1948, Clipping File, Fine Arts Collection, St. Louis Public Library.

74. Minutes, 30 August 1948, B'nai Amoona Archives.

75. E. Millstone, interview with the author, June 1998. According to advertisements placed in the *Jewish Record*, 30 September 1950, and the *National Jewish Post*, 25 August 1950, the subcontractors included Campbell Lathing and Plaster Company; Fox Brothers Manufacturing Company; Frank Kirk and Sons, who did the brick work; Mack Electric Company; J. Pellarin and Company, the terrazo contractor; Richards-Wilcox Manufacturing Company, who supplied the folding doors; J. Sheehan Plumbing Company; Edward C. Simon Painting Company; and United Lumber Company.

76. Peters, "A Great Architect's Vision."

77. "Our Dream Comes True," B'nai Amoona Archives.

78. There are also a number of preliminary sketches for these drawings, which highlights the importance Mendelsohn accorded them. See Zevi, *Complete Works*, 305, fig. 15; 306, figs. 2–5; and 308, fig. 2.

79. Eric to Louise Mendelsohn, letter of 7 November 1947, Mendelsohn Archive.

80. Minutes, 1 November 1948, B'nai Amoona archives.

81. Minutes, 2 May, 6 June, and 6 November 1949, B'nai Amoona Archives. See also Bronson, *B'nai Amoona*, 148.

82. Eric to Louise Mendelsohn, letter of 26 June 1950, Mendelsohn Archive.

83. Eric to Louise Mendelsohn, letter of 15 September 1950, Mendelsohn Archive.

84. "Our Dream Comes True," B'nai Amoona Archives.

85. Quoted in Bronson, *B'nai Amoona*, 151.

86. Bernard S. Raskas, *A Son of Faith: From the Sermons of Abraham E. Halpern, 1891–1962* (New York: Bloch Publishing Company, 1962), 84.

87. Carol Herselle Krinsky, *The Synagogues of Europe* (New York: Architectural History Foundation, 1985).

88. Mendelsohn, "In the Spirit of Our Age," 541.

89. Johannes van Acken, *Christozentrische Kirchenkunst: Ein Entwurf zum Liturgischen-Gesamtkunstwerk* (Gladbeck i. W.: A. Theben, 1923, 2d ed.), and Bartning, *Vom neuen Kirchbau*, for the initial articulation of these principles. Willy Weyres and Otto Bartning, eds., *Kirchen: Handbuch für den Kirchenbau* (München: Verlage Georg D. W. Callwey: 1959) contains an important postwar summary of these beliefs. For their impact,

see Albert Christ-Janer and Mary Mix Foley, *Modern Church Architecture: A Guide to the Form and Spirit of 20th Century Religious Buildings* (New York: McGraw-Hill Book Company, Inc., 1962), and Robert Maguire and Keith Murray, *Modern Churches of the World* (London: Studio Vista Limited, 1965).

90. Kaufman, *Shul with a Pool*.

91. Edward S. Shapiro, *A Time for Healing: American Jewry Since World War II* (Baltimore: The Johns Hopkins University Press, 1992), 147–51, and Jack Westheimer, *The American Synagogue: A Sanctuary Transformed* (Cambridge: Cambridge University Press, 1987), 125.

92. This is the view that was most often published.

93. Quoted in Bronson, *B'nai Amoona*, 151.

94. Eric to Louise Mendelsohn, letter of 15 September 1950, Mendelsohn Archive.

95. Bronson, *B'nai Amoona*, 150.

96. For instance, the drawing published in Zevi, *Complete Works*, 305, fig. 13, as well as a number of the plan drawings for the building's principal floor. All are in the Mendelsohn Archive.

97. Bronson, *B'nai Amoona*, 155.

98. Robert E. Hannon, "Contemporary Synagogue: A Structure by a Famous Architect and for University City Congregation," *St. Louis Post-Dispatch*, 24 December 1950, Pictures Supplement, 5.

99. Ibid.

100. "Eric Mendelsohn," *Architectural Forum* 86 (May 1947): 76; and "Synagogue in St. Louis, Mo.," *Architectural Forum* 98 (April 1953): 109–15.

101. Judy Little, *University City: Landmarks and Historic Places* (University City: Historic Preservation Commission), 45, 49. "New Synagogue in University City Being Erected," clipping dated 13 May 1951, clipping files, Fine Arts Department, St. Louis Public Library.

102. John T. Stewart, "Dunn's Design for Faith-Salem Evangelical and Reformed Congregation, Jennings," *St. Louis Post-Dispatch*, 24 October 1951.

103. "The New Look in Churches," *St. Louis Globe-Democrat*, Sunday Magazine, 16 March 1958.

104. *L'architecture d'aujourd'hui* 71 (April/May 1957) was devoted to new religious architecture. The Resurrection church was illustrated on page 61; B'nai Amoona on page 76.

105. Dedication of Resurrection Church, 20 June 1954, program preserved in the clipping files, Fine Arts Department, St. Louis Public Library.

106. "The New Look in Churches."

107. Rachel Wischnitzer-Bernstein, "The Problem of Synagogue Architecture: Creating a Style Expressive of America," *Commentary* 3 (1947): 241.

108. Zevi, *Opera Completa* 310–30, 342–47, 364–83, 386–93; Whittick, *Mendelsohn*, 146–69; and Morganthaler, "Arbeiten in den USA," in Stephan, *Mendelsohn*, 297–312. Zevi also published Mendelsohn's preliminary sketches for congregations in Providence, Rhode Island, and Miami, Florida.

109. Mendelsohn to Packman, letter of 9 November 1945, Mendelsohn Archive.

110. Walter Leedy, "Eric Mendelsohn's Park Synagogue: Vision Informs Reality," *Gamut* (Cleveland: Cleveland State University Press, 1989), 45–69.

111. "Noted Architect Washington University Guest," *St. Louis Post Dispatch*, 19 February 1950.

112. James, *Mendelsohn*, 195–97, and 203, for an earlier chapter in the competitive relationship between the two.

113. Eric to Louise Mendelsohn, letter of 27 January 1950, Mendelsohn Archive.

114. Eric to Louise Mendelsohn, letter of 31 January 1950, Mendelsohn Archive.

115. Gail Fenske, "Lewis Mumford, Henry-Russell Hitchcock, and the Bay Region Style," in Martha Pollak, ed., *The Education of the Architect: Historiography, Urbanism, and the Growth of Architectural Knowledge* (Cambridge: MIT Press, 1997), 37–85, and Marc Treib, ed., *An Everyday Modernism: The Houses of William Wurster* (Berkeley: University of California Press, 1995).

116. Eric Mendelsohn to Victor Packman, letter of 20 November Mendelsohn Archive.

117. See Elizabeth Mock, *Built in USA: 1932–1944* (New York: Museum of Modern Art, 1944).

118. Mendelsohn's clipping file is in the Documents Collection, College of Environmental Design, University of California, Berkeley.

119. Peter Winston, interview with the author, June 1998. The high cost of the steel frame was one of the objections Edith Farnsworth had to the house Mies built for her in Plano, Illinois. See Alice Friedman, *Women and the Making of the Modern House* (New York: Abbeville, 1998), 140. Unpublished drawings for the Winston House, 1946, remain in a private collection.

120. Eric to Louise Mendelsohn, letter of 12 March 1946, Mendelsohn Archive.

121. Ibid.

122. Eric to Louise Mendelsohn, letter of 2 May 1947, Mendelsohn Archive.

123. Wolf van Eckhardt, *Eric Mendelsohn* (New York: Braziller, 1960), 13.

124. Peters, "A Great Architect's Vision."

125. Publications focusing on Jewish art and architecture in which B'nai Amoona features prominently include Peter Blake, ed., *An American Synagogue for Today and Tomorrow* (New York: The Union of American Hebrew Congregations, 1954), 99–102; Edward Jamilly, "The Architecture of the Contemporary Synagogue," in Cecil Roth, ed., *Jewish Art: An Illustrated History* (New York: McGraw-Hill, 1961), 788; and Avram Kampf, *Contemporary Synagogue Art: Developments in the United States, 1945–65* (New York: Union of American Hebrew Congregations, 1966), 31, 174–76. More recent histories of synagogue architecture focus on the postwar buildings erected by better-remembered gentile architects.

126. Newspaper clipping dated 13 March 1957, collection of I. E. Millstone, whose firm were the contractors.

127. Frank Peters, "Erich Mendelsohn's Legacy to St. Louis," *St. Louis Post-Dispatch*, 4 September 1983, 5F, and Peters, "A Great Architect's Vision."

128. Frank Peters, "Erich Mendelsohn's Modern Synagogue Enters New Life as a Cultural Center," *St. Louis Post-Dispatch*, 12 October 1986, 5C.

PORTFOL

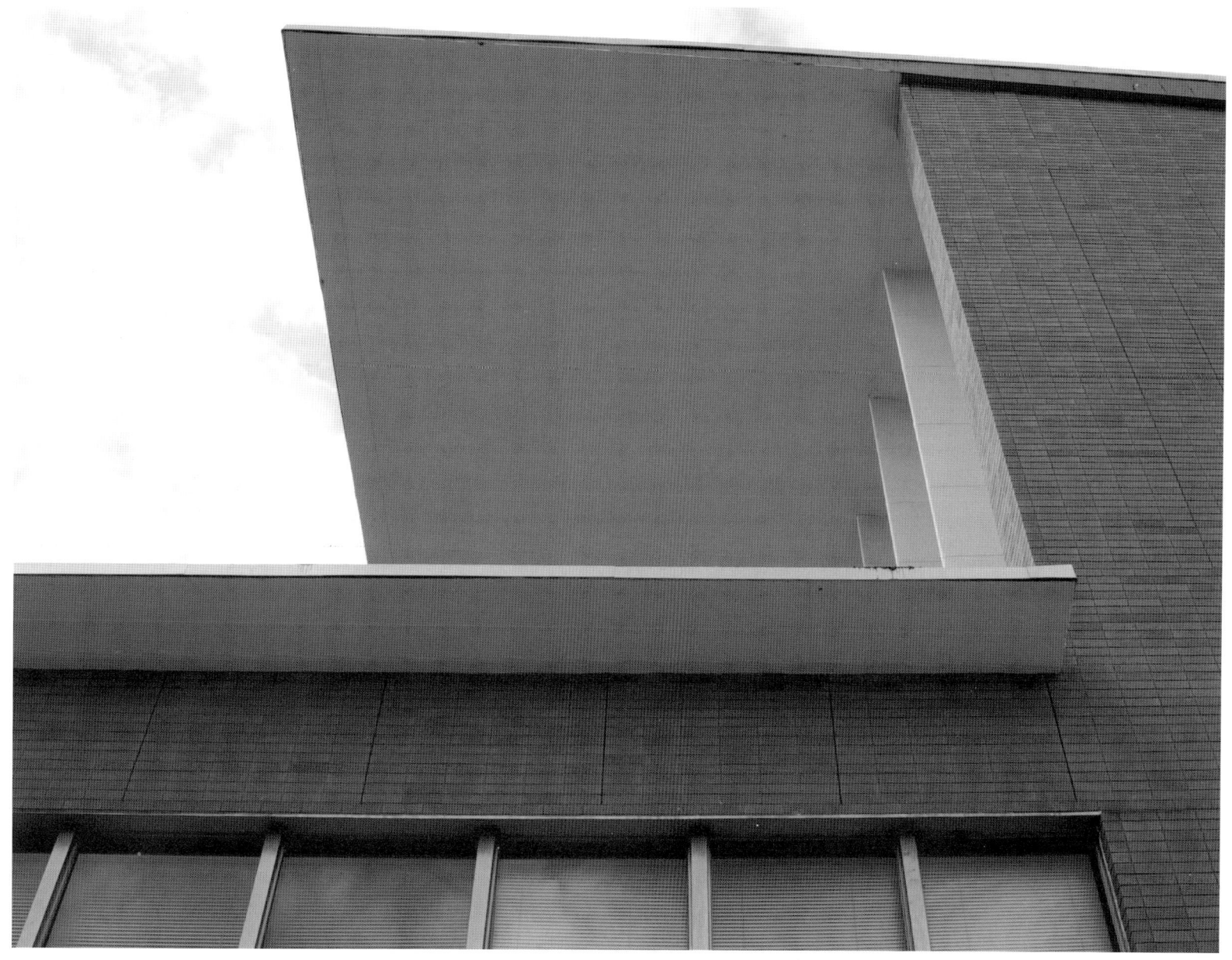

Typefaces: Helvetica and Bodoni   *Paper:* Warren Lustro Dull, 100 lb. Text

Archive photographs were scanned at 300 dpi and printed as 150 line duotones. Photographer Gen Obata used digital cameras for the contemporary images.